MACBETH

By WILLIAM SHAKESPEARE

Preface and Annotations by
HENRY N. HUDSON

Introduction by
CHARLES HAROLD HERFORD

Read by
ELIZABETH A. VANIER

Macbeth
By William Shakespeare
Preface and Annotations by Henry N. Hudson
Introduction by Charles Harold Herford

Print ISBN 13: 978-1-4209-5218-6
eBook ISBN 13: 978-1-4209-5219-3

Cover Image: Macbeth (oil on canvas), Chasseriau, Theodore (1819-56) / Musee des Beaux-Arts, Valenciennes, France, / Bridgeman Images.

Please visit *www.digireads.com*

CONTENTS

MACBETH

Preface

First printed in the folio of 1623. On the 8th of November, that year, it was registered at the Stationers" by Blount and Jaggard, as one of the plays "not formerly entered to other men."

The text of this drama has come down to us in a state far from satisfactory. Though not so badly printed as some other plays in the same volume, for instance, *All's Well that Ends Well* and *Coriolanus*, still it has a number of very troublesome passages. In several cases, the errors are of such a nature that we can hardly refer them to any other than a phonographic origin. On this point, the learned editors of the Clarendon edition observe as follows: "Probably it was printed from a transcript of the author's manuscript, which was in great part not copied from the original, but written to dictation. This is confirmed by the fact that several of the most palpable blunders are blunders of the ear, and not of the eye."

The minute and searching criticism of our time has made out, almost, if not altogether, beyond question, that considerable portions of *Macbeth* were not written by Shakespeare. I have been very slow and reluctant to admit this conclusion; but the evidence, it seems to me, is not to be withstood. It is, moreover, highly probable. to say the least, that few of the scenes, perhaps none, have reached us altogether in the form they received from the Poet's hand. But, as this matter is to be discussed under the heading "Shakespeare and Middleton," and as the lines judged not to be Shakespeare's are asterized in this edition, it need not be enlarged upon here.

The date of the composition has been variously argued and concluded. Until a recent period, there was nothing but internal evidence at hand for settling the date. Proceeding upon this, Malone and Chalmers agreed upon the year 1606 as the *probable* time of the writing. That the composition was subsequent to the union of the English and Scottish crowns, was justly inferred from what the hero says in his last interview with the Weird Sisters: "And some I see, that twofold dolls and *treble sceptres* carry." James the First came to the throne of England in March, 1603; but the two crowns were not formally united, at least the union was not proclaimed, till October, 1604.

Our earliest authentic notice of *Macbeth* is from one Simon Forman, M.D., an astrologer, quack, and dealer in the arts of magic, who kept a sort of diary which he entitled *The Book of Plays and Notes thereof.* In 1836 the manuscript of this diary was discovered in the Ashmolean Museum, and a portion of its contents published. Forman gives a somewhat minute and particular account of the plot and leading incidents of the drama, as he saw it played at the Globe theatre on

Saturday the 20th of April, 1610. The passage is too long for my space; but it is a very mark-worthy circumstance, that from the way it begins, and from the wording of it, we should naturally infer that what now stands as the first scene of the play, then made no part of the performance. The passage opens thus: "In Macbeth, at the Globe, 1610. the 20th of April, Saturday, there was to be observed, first, how Macbeth and Banquo, two noblemen of Scotland, riding through a wood, there stood before them three women, faries or nymphs, and saluted Macbeth, saying three times unto him, Hail," &c.

It is highly probable, to say the least, that the tragedy was then fresh from the Poet's hand, and was in its first course of ' performance. Some arguments, indeed, or seeming arguments, have been adduced, inferring the play to have been written three or four years earlier; but I can see no great force in them. On the other hand, it appears that Forman had long been an habitual frequenter of play-houses; and it seems nowise likely that one so eager in quest of novelties would either have missed the play, had it been put upon the stage before, or have made so special a notice of it, but that he then saw it for the first time. Nor have the characteristics of the work itself any thing to say against the date in question; those portions of it that have the clearest and most unquestionable impress of Shakespeare's hand being in his greatest, richest, most idiomatic style.

The story of Macbeth, as it lived in tradition, had been told by Holinshed, whose *Chronicles* first appeared in 1577, and by George Buchanan, the learned preceptor of James the First, who has been termed the Scotch Livy, and whose *History of Scotland* came forth in 1582. The main features of the story, so far as it is adopted by the Poet, are the same in both these writers, save that Buchanan represents Macbeth to have merely dreamed of meeting the Weird Sisters, and of being hailed by them successively as Thane of Angus, Thane of Murray, and as King. Holinshed was Shakespeare's usual authority in matters of British history. In the present case the Poet shows no traces of obligation to Buchanan, unless, which is barely possible, he may have taken a hint from the historian, where the latter, speaking of Macbeth's reign, says, "Certain of our writers here relate many idle things which I omit, as being fitter for Milesian fables or *for the theatre* than for sober history." A passage which, as showing the author's care for the truth of what he wrote, perhaps should make us wary of trusting too much in later writers, who would have us believe that, a war of factions breaking out, Duncan was killed In battle, and Macbeth took the crown by just and lawful title. And it is considerable that both Hume and Lingard acquiesce in the old account which represents Macbeth to have murdered Duncan, and usurped the throne.

According to the history, Malcolm, King of Scotland, had two daughters, Beatrice and Doada, severally married to Abanath Crinen and to Sinel, Thanes of the Isles and of Glamis, by whom each had a son named Duncan and Macbeth. The former succeeded his grandfather in the kingdom; and, he being of a soft and gentle disposition, his reign was at first very quiet and peaceable, but afterwards, by reason of his slackness, was greatly harassed with troubles and seditions, wherein his cousin, who was valiant and warlike, did great service to the State.

I condense the main particulars of the historic matter. After narrating the victory of the Scottish generals over the rebels and invaders, the chronicler proceeds in substance as follows:

Macbeth and Banquo were on their way to Forres, where the King then lay; and, as they were passing through the fields alone, three women in strange and wild attire suddenly met them; and, while they were rapt with wonder at the sight, the first said, "All hail, Macbeth, Thane of Glamis"; the second, "Hail, Macbeth, Thane of Cawdor"; the third, "Hail, Macbeth, that hereafter shalt be King." Then said Banquo, "What manner of women are you, that to my fellow here, besides high offices, ye assign the kingdom, but promise nothing to me?" "Yes," said the first, "we promise greater things to thee: for he shall reign indeed, but shall have no issue to succeed him; whereas thou indeed shalt not reign, but from thee shall spring a long line of kings." Then the women immediately vanished. At first the men thought this was but a fantastical illusion, insomuch that Banquo would call Macbeth king in jest, and Macbeth in like sort would call him father of many kings. But afterwards the women were believed to be the Weird Sisters; because, the Thane of Cawdor being condemned for treason, his lands and titles were given to Macbeth. Whereupon Banquo said to him jestingly, "Now, Macbeth, thou hast what two of the Sisters promised; there remaineth only what the other said should come to pass." And Macbeth began even then to devise how he might come to the throne, but thought he must wait for time to work his way, as in the former preferment. But when, shortly after, the King made his oldest son Prince of Cumberland, thereby in effect appointing him successor, Macbeth was sorely troubled thereat, as it seemed to cut off his hope; and, thinking the purpose was to defeat his title to the crown, he studied to usurp it by force. Encouraged by the words of the Weird Sisters, and urged on by his wife, who was "burning with unquenchable desire to bear the name of queen," he at length whispered his design to some trusty friends, and, having a promise of their aid, slew the King at Inverness; then got himself proclaimed king, and forthwith went to Scone, where, by common consent, he was invested after the usual manner.

The circumstances of the murder, as set forth in the play, were taken from another part of the history, where Holinshed relates how King Duff, being the guest of Donwald and his wife in their castle at Forres, was there murdered. The story ran as follows: King Duff having retired for the rest of the night, his two chamberlains, as soon as they saw him well a-bed, came forth, and fell to banqueting with Donwald and his wife, who had prepared many choice dishes and drinks for their rear-supper; wherewith they so gorged themselves, that their heads no sooner got to the pillow than they were so fast asleep that the chamber might have been removed without waking them. Then Donwald, goaded on by his wife, though in heart he greatly abhorred the act, called four of his servants, whom he had already framed to the purpose with large gifts; and they, entering the King's chamber, cut his throat as he lay asleep, and carried the body forth into the fields. In the morning, a noise being made that the King was slain, Donwald ran thither with the watch, as though he knew nothing of it, and, finding cakes of blood in the bed and on the floor, forthwith slew the chamberlains as guilty of the murder.

The body of Duncan was conveyed to Colmekill, and there laid in a sepulchre amongst his predecessors, in the year 1040. Malcolm and Donalbain, the sons of Duncan, for fear of their lives fled into Cumberland, where Malcolm remained till Saint Edward recovered England from the Danish power. Edward received Malcolm with most friendly entertainment, but Donalbain passed over into Ireland, where he was tenderly cherished by the King of that land,

Macbeth, after the departure of Duncan's sons, used great liberality towards the nobles of the realm, thereby to win their favour; and, when he saw that no man went about to trouble him, he set his whole endeavour to maintain justice, and to punish all enormities and abuses which had chanced through the feeble administration of Duncan. He continued governing the realm for the space of ten years in equal justice; but this was but a. counterfeit zeal, to purchase thereby the favour of the people. Shortly after, he began to show what he was, practising cruelty instead of equity. For the prick of conscience caused him ever to fear, lest he should be served with the same cup as he had ministered to his predecessor. The words, also, of the Weird Sisters would not out of his mind; which, as they promised him the kingdom, did likewise promise it at the same time to the posterity of Banquo. He therefore desired Banquo and his son named Fleance to come to a supper that he had prepared for them; but hired certain murderers to meet them without the palace as they returned to their lodgings, and there to slay them. Yet it chanced, by the benefit of the dark night, that, though the father was slain, the son escaped that danger; and afterwards, having some inkling how his life was sought no less than his father's, to avoid further peril he fled into Wales.

After the slaughter of Banquo, nothing prospered with Macbeth. For every man began to doubt his own life, and durst hardly appear in the King's presence; and as there were many that stood in fear of him, so likewise stood he in fear of many, in such sort that he began to make those away whom he thought most able to work him any displeasure. At length he found such sweetness in putting his nobles to death, that his thirst after blood might nowise be satisfied. For, first, they were rid out of the way whom he feared; then, his coffers were enriched by their goods, whereby he might the better maintain a guard of armed men about him, to defend his person from them whom he had in any suspicion.

To the end he might the more safely oppress his subjects, he built a strong castle on the top of a high hill called Dunsinane. This castle put the realm to great expense, before it was finished; for all the stuff necessary to the building could not be brought up without much toil and business. But Macbeth, being determined to have the work go forward, caused the thanes of each shire within the realm to come and help towards the building, each man his course about. At last, when the turn fell to Macduff, Thane of Fife, he sent workmen with all needful provision, and commanded them to show such diligence, that no occasion might be given for the King to find fault with him for not coming himself; which he refused to do for fear lest the King should lay violent hands upon him, as he had done upon divers others.

Shortly after, Macbeth, coming to behold how the work went forward, was sore offended because he found not Macduff there, and said, "I perceive this man will never obey my commands till he be ridden with a snaffle; but I shall provide enough for him." Nor could he afterwards abide to look upon Macduff, either because he thought his puissance over-great, or else because he had learned of certain wizards, in whose words he put great confidence, that he ought to take heed of Macduff. And surely he had put Macduff to death, but that a certain witch, in whom he had great trust, had told him he should never be slain by a man born of any woman, nor be vanquished till the wood of Birnam came to the castle of Dunsinane. By this prophecy Macbeth put all fear out of his heart, supposing he might do what he would. This vain hope caused him to do many outrageous things, to the grievous oppression of his subjects.

At length Macduff, to avoid peril of life, purposed with himself to pass into England, to procure Malcolm to claim the crown of Scotland. But this was not so secretly devised, but that Macbeth had knowledge thereof: for he had, in every nobleman's house, one sly fellow or other in fee with him, to reveal all that was said or done within the same. Immediately then, being informed where Macduff went, he came hastily with a great power into Fife, and forthwith besieged the castle where Macduff dwelt, trusting to find him therein. They that kept the house opened the gates without any resistance, mistrusting no evil. Nevertheless Macbeth most cruelly caused the wife and children of Macduff, with all others whom he found in the castle, to be slain. He also confiscated the goods of Macduff, and proclaimed him traitor; but

Macduff had already escaped out of danger, and gone into England to Malcolm, to try what he could do, by his support, to revenge the slaughter of his wife, his children, and other friends.

Holinshed then proceeds to relate, at considerable length, the interview between Macduff and Malcolm at the English Court, setting forth the particulars of their talk in the same order, and partly in the same words, as we have them in the Poet's text.

Soon after, Macduff, repairing to the borders of Scotland, addressed letters with secret dispatch to the nobles of the realm, declaring how Malcolm was confederate with him, to come hastily into Scotland to claim the crown. In the meantime, Malcolm gained such favour at King Edward's hands, that old Siward, Earl of Northumberland, was appointed with ten thousand men to go with him into Scotland, to support him in this enterprise. After this news was spread abroad in Scotland, the nobles drew into several factions, the one taking part with Macbeth, the other with Malcolm.

When Macbeth perceived his enemies" power to increase by such aid as came to them out of England, he fell back into Fife, purposing to abide at the Castle of Dunsinane, and to fight with his enemies, if they meant to pursue him. Malcolm, following hastily after Macbeth, came the night before the battle to Birnam wood; and, when his army had rested awhile there, he commanded every man to get a bough of some tree of that wood in his hand, as big as he might bear, and to march forth therewith in such wise, that on the next morning they might come closely within view of his enemies.

On the morrow, when Macbeth beheld them coming in this sort, he first marvelled what the matter meant; but in the end remembered himself, that the prophecy, which he had heard long before, of the coming of Birnam wood to Dunsinane-Castle, was likely now to be fulfilled. Nevertheless he brought his men in order of battle, and exhorted them to do valiantly; howbeit his enemies had scarcely cast from them their boughs, when Macbeth, perceiving their numbers, betook him straight to flight. Macduff pursued him with great hatred, till Macbeth, perceiving that he was hard at his back, leaped beside his horse, saying, "Thou traitor, what meaneth it that thou shouldst thus in vain follow me, who am not appointed to be slain by any creature that is born of a woman: come on, therefore, and receive thy reward"; and therewithal he lifted up his sword, thinking to have slain him. But Macduff, quickly leaping from his horse, answered, with his naked sword in his hand, "It is true, Macbeth; and now shall thy insatiable cruelty have an end: for I am even he that thy wizards told thee of, who was never born of my mother, but ripped out of her womb": therewithal he stepped unto him, and slew him. Then, cutting his head from his shoulders, he set it upon a pole, and brought it to Malcolm. This was the end of Macbeth, after he had reigned seventeen years over the

Scottishmen.

HENRY N. HUDSON

Introduction

Macbeth was first published in the Folio of 1623. It is there already divided into scenes as well as acts. In other respects it is carelessly edited, and the text is among the worst printed in the entire series. In addition, the 'perfect' and 'absolute' copy of Shakespeare's work, which the editors of the Folio professed to print, is open to grave suspicion of having been severely revised, cut down, and interpolated after it left his hands. Much, finally, of what is unmistakably Shakespearean has rather the qualities of bold blocking out than of finished workmanship. Verses otherwise stamped with genius jostle rudely with every canon of metre, and the magnificent and inexhaustible poetry forces its way through daring anomalies of speech; while the supreme dramatic energy is focused upon the two or three principal characters, with an exclusive intensity more characteristic of Æschylus than of the myriad-minded author of world dramas like *Lear* and *Hamlet.* Under conditions so complex as these, the textual criticism of *Macbeth* is inevitably beset with problems which our knowledge does not suffice to solve.

The theory of a post-Shakespearean revision of *Macbeth* starts from a slender but definite basis of fact. Middleton's *The Witch* contains two songs referred to in the stage directions of *Macbeth* (viz. 'Come away, come away,' iii. 5., and 'Black spirits and white, iv. i.), and afterwards introduced in Davenant's recast of his godfather's work. *The Witch* was most likely written some years after *Macbeth*; it was certainly old when *Macbeth* was printed. The coincidence can be accounted for on several hypotheses, as Mr. Bullen has shown; but the presumption decidedly is that the songs, simply referred to by their first lines in *Macbeth*, as familiar, were drawn from the play where they are quoted in full. This presumption gives a certain *locus standi* to theories of more extensive interpolation, which have been freely advanced with very various degrees of critical competency. The more revolutionary proposals of Messrs. Clark and Wright[1] have found support only from Mr. Fleay, who has since withdrawn it.[2] Besides a large part of the witch scenes, which might be plausibly assigned to the author of *The Witch*, and the porter scene, which had been rejected by Coleridge, they condemned the 'Serjeant scene' (i. 2.), the king's-evil scene (iv. 3. 140-

---

[1] Edition of *Macbeth*, Introduction (Clar. Press Series).
[2] In the *Life and Work of Shakespeare*, p. 238, Mr. Fleay rejects only iii. 5. and iv. 1. 39-43.

159), the relation of young Siward's death and crowning of Malcolm (v. 8. 35-75), and a variety of rhyming tags. The only serious allegation against the Serjeant scene is that it relates the treason of Cawdor, which in the following scene is still unknown to Macbeth (i. 3. 72), and doubtful to Angus (i. 3. in). But this 'discrepancy' is of the kind that arises when explanatory links drop out; it points rather to compression than to interpolation, and cannot for a moment avail against the profusion of Shakespearean touches scattered through both. That the porter scene, too, is in conception and execution altogether Shakespearean few recent critics doubt; for us, as for De Quincey,[3] the stage resolves the hesitation of the study; and the lofty morning-hymn which Schiller provided for the German people in place of these less edifying reflections has disappeared even from the German stage.[4] The question thus reduces itself to the witch scenes. It must La allowed that there are here striking discrepancies of tone. In part, however, this means merely that in the witches, being a Shakespearean fusion of beings very unlike in legendary character, now the more poetic and now the grosser traits are dominant. But this does not hold of the strangely incongruous figure of Hecate. The leader and controller of the witches in Middleton's play had naturally no place in the legend of Macbeth. She is introduced for the first time in iii. 5. to ask the reason of her exclusion; but to the end she is a palpable intruder in the witches' cavern. With her entrance the northern scenery is suddenly brought into relation with classic myth; they are to meet her, no more on the blasted heath, but at the pit of Acheron; while the language, released from the weird horror or grossness of the other witch scenes, trips along in courtly rococo elegance, with graceful artifices of fancy suggestive of the *Midsummer-Night's Dream.* Her conceptions of enchantment belong to the world of Oberon; she proposes to beguile Macbeth with the distillations of a vaporous drop that hangs upon a corner of the moon; and the wild, withered hags about the cauldron remind her of elves and fairies in a ring. Of her enchantments nothing more is heard. The apparitions that fatally palter with Macbeth are raised by no lunar dewdrop, but by the less ethereal ingredients of the cauldron; and Hecate's naive applause (iv. i. 39-43) does not disguise her complete insignificance and superfluity. To these two passages of extremely doubtful authenticity may probably be added the farewell speech of the First Witch in the same scene (iv. 1. 125-132), whose good-natured desire to 'cheer up his sprites' is so oddly out of keeping

---

[3] *On the Knocking at the Gate in Macbeth.* Cf. Prof. Hales' full discussion of the whole question: *The Porter in Macbeth* (N. Shaksp. Soc. Transactions, 1874).

[4] Schiller's adaptation of *Macbeth* appeared at Weimar in 1800. It is open to, and has received, severe criticism; but many of its defects spring from excessive regard for the immature taste of his public rather than from his own, and his version contributed enormously to domesticate Shakespeare in Germany.

with their character as demoniac contrivers of harm, and with the 'horrible sight' they have just disclosed to 'grieve his heart.' It may be noted, too, that all three passages *(i.e.* iii. 5., iv. 1. 39-43, and 125-132), are composed in iambic verse, the rest of the witch scenes being all trochaic.[5]

Putting aside these passages (about forty lines) *Macbeth* can be assigned with some assurance to 1606. The unmistakable allusions to James (the 'two-fold balls and treble sceptres,' iv. 1. 119-122, and the touching for the king's evil, a treasured prerogative of his, iv. 3. 140-159) were of course written after his accession, and would lose point had his accession not been comparatively recent. The choice of subject implied, in effect, a double compliment to the king. Academic ingenuity had already brought the prophecies of the weird sisters into relation with the demonological descendant of Banquo; his entry into Oxford in 1605 having been celebrated in prophetic verses addressed to him by three students in the character of Witches.[6] The Porter, again, in his quality of Clown, founds allusive jests on topics of 1606: the phenomenally abundant harvest (ii. 3. 5), and the Jesuit Garnet's defence of equivocation at his trial in the spring (iv. 3. 10). On the other hand, the play was already familiar in 1607, for Middleton's *The Puritan* contains an evident reference to Banquo's ghost: 'Instead of a jester we'll have a ghost in a white sheet sit at the upper end of the table.' It is also significant that Warner in 1606 inserted a *Historie of Macbeth* in a new edition of his popular repertory of English history, *Albion's England.* An unquestionable later limit is furnished by Dr. Simon Forman's account of the performance of *Macbeth* which he witnessed at the Globe in 1610. The curious naïveté of his report of the plot persuaded the older editors that the play must have been new. It was doubtless new to him.

No earlier handling of the story of Macbeth can be clearly made out. A ballad on 'Macdobeth' was entered in 1596 in the Stationers' Register, and Kempe, four years later, contemptuously referred to 'the miserable story of Mac-doel, or Mac-dobeth, or Macsomewhat' (*Nine Days' Wonder,* 1600). Whatever may lurk under these ambiguous allusions, it is clear that Shakespeare drew his materials substantially from Holinshed's *Chronicle of England and Scotland,* the long-familiar source of his English Histories and of *King Lear.* Even as told by Holinshed, the story is very great, and Shakespeare, in the very maturity of his art, found little to change or to add. In this, as in most other points of technique, *Macbeth* stands at the opposite pole to *King*

---

[5] Cf. the excellent discussion of the supposed interpolations by Mr. E. K. Chambers in his edition of the play for the Warwick Series (Appendices E, F, G), to which I owe some suggestions.

[6] James's *Demonologie,* an elaborate refutation of free-thinking in matters of witchcraft, and especially of the sceptic Reginald Scot, appeared in 1599.

Lear. No parallel from modern romance (like the Gloucester story from the *Arcadia)* crosses and complicates the ancient legendary theme: Macbeth and his wife fill the entire field without reflexion or counterpart. It is clear, nevertheless, that Shakespeare, though he may have thought the story as historical as that of the Richards or Henries, no longer approached it as history. Macbeth's career, and to some extent his character, are modelled on those of another Scottish assassin, Donwald, whose treacherous murder of King Duff Holinshed had described in vivid detail some twenty pages before, while of Duncan's murder he recorded merely the bare fact. Donwald, an officer of the king, enjoying his absolute trust, entertained him in the castle of Fores, of which he had charge. His wife incited him to use his opportunity, 'and shewed him the means whereby he might soonest accomplish it.'[7] Donwald himself 'abhorred the act greatly in heart,' but yields to his wife's urgency. Duff on retiring sends a present to his host; the grooms in the king's chamber, plied with meat and drink by his wife's care, sleep heavily, and fall victims, next morning, to Donwald's 'pious rage.' Fearful portents ensue: the sun is darkened; birds and beasts run counter to their common instincts. All these details Shakespeare has transferred to the story of Duncan, and they add greatly to its tragic force. Holinshed's Macbeth is only his victim's 'kinsman and his subject'; Shakespeare's violates a yet stronger instinct as 'his host,' 'who should against his murderer shut the door, not bear the knife himself.' Holinshed's Macbeth plans and executes the murder with matter-of-fact promptitude, without a trace of hesitation or compunction; Shakespeare's Macbeth, like Donwald, has accesses of deep reluctance, in which his wife's resolute energy turns the scale. Holinshed's Lady Macbeth urges her husband 'to attempt the thing,' but has no part in its execution. Thus the elements of the relation between Macbeth and Lady Macbeth, and of the hesitations and 'infirmity' which chiefly make him a tragic figure at all, are suggested by Holinshed's Donwald, not by his Macbeth. Much even of the political background of the murder belongs rather to the story of Duff. Holinshed's Macbeth acts with the complicity of 'his trusty friends,'— Banquo among the rest,—and 'upon confidence of their promised aid' Shakespeare's Macbeth, like Donwald, has no political confederates, can count upon no sympathy if his part in the 'deep damnation' of the king's 'taking off' is discovered, and precipitates discovery by overacting his feigned grief.[8] Even Donwald has the aid of trusty

---

[7] Stone's *Holinshed,* p. 26 f. It is interesting to note that Milton included both 'Macbeth' and 'Duff and Donwald' in his list of subjects for a tragedy. It is clear that he would have kept the two stories wholly distinct. In a valuable and suggestive paper Prof. Hales has indicated the lines on which the poet of *Paradise Lost* would probably have treated the Temptation and Fall of Macbeth (*Folia Litteraria,* 198 f.).

[8] Donwald, as already stated, slays the chamberlains. And such, Holinshed

servants: Shakespeare sends husband and wife unaided to their work amid the cry of owls and the prayers of startled sleepers. Finally, Shakespeare has deprived Macbeth of the shadow of political justification which his prototype in Holinshed might plead for his crime. Holinshed's Duncan is a gentle weakling, whom the rebel Macdonwald openly taunts as a 'faint-hearted milksop, more meet to govern a sect of idle monks in some cloister than to have the rule of such valiant and hardy men of war as the Scots were.' He is helplessly dependent upon his great captains, Macbeth and Banquho, and holds his kingdom only by their aid; while Macbeth, having got rid of him, gives Scotland for ten years the blessing of a strong, just rule. Shakespeare's Duncan has all the graces of this type without its defects, bearing his faculties 'meekly,' but 'clear in his great office'; and Macbeth, valiant and loyal soldier as he appears at the outset, is hurried from his first act of 'foul play,' without an instant's pause, and with ever increasing velocity, down the abyss of crime.

Thus Shakespeare prepares the ground for his tragedy of crime by clearing away all its normal pretexts and palliations. No film of finer motive softens its essential baseness. Alone among the heroes of Shakespeare's mature tragedy, Macbeth murders with the vulgar cupidity of the common cut-throat. Vulgar cupidity is not, taken by itself, a tragic motive; and the stupendous effect of this drama has nothing in common with the pathos which springs from the interworking of a man's noble frailties with his fate, as in *Othello* or *Hamlet*. In a very marvellous way Shakespeare has contrived, without using other than mean motives as the impelling forces of the action, yet to connect it with permanent realities, to give it that 'semblance of eternity' without which great art cannot exist. The two criminal figures are lifted into tragic significance by a strange intensity of mental vision, which, while it does not preclude them from vulgar crime, makes them capable of a nowise vulgar Nemesis. Macbeth has much of the mental habitude of Hamlet. He has the feverish activity of intellect, which turns the common dust of daily incident and impulse into fiery trains of imagery and reflexion, and calls up his own past and purposed acts in spectral visions—a bloody dagger, a sheeted ghost—before his eyes. In Macbeth, as in Hamlet, the mental tumult tends to retard action; his 'flighty purpose never is o'ertook unless the deed go with it.' But the tragic effect lies no longer in the visions which retard his action, but in those which revenge it. Hamlet is wrought into accesses of passion when confronted with the practical energy which he lacks, and Macbeth, ruthless as he is, has a preternaturally acute sense of the

---

proceeds, 'was his over-earnest diligence in the severe inquisition and trial of the offenders herein, that some of the lords began to mislike the matter, and to smell for the shrewd tokens that he should not be altogether clear himself." Cf. Lennox's ironical account of Macbeth's 'grief' (iii. 6.).

power of pity. He foresees it 'striding the blast' and blowing 'the horrid deed in every eye, that tears shall drown the wind' Day itself is 'pitiful,' and night shall scarf up her 'tender eye' before the murder of Banquo. The most appalling glimpses do not deter Macbeth from action any more than they prompt Hamlet to it; but they prey upon him when it is over. Here his wife's sensibility is as keen as his; and if it is less fiercely tossed into images, it is crueler and more corroding. Both loathe their power as soon as they have it; and we hear the groan involuntarily wrung from each without the other's knowledge (iii. 2.). Hers is the groan of the parched throat craving water and tasting dust:—

> Nought's had, all's spent,
> Where our desire is got without content:
> 'Tis safer to be that which we destroy
> Than by destruction dwell in doubtful joy.

His expresses the delirium of mental torture, 'the affliction of these terrible dreams that shake us nightly':—

> better be with the dead,
> Whom we, to gain our peace, have sent to peace,
> Than on the torture of the mind to lie
> In restless ecstasy.

Neither feels remorse, but the sense of unatoned guilt haunts them in eerie visions of indelible bloodstains. With her the thought breaks forth only in the mental dissolution of her dreams, and in a quite simple form: 'All the perfumes of Arabia will not sweeten this little hand.' With him its horror is never absent, and it utters itself in a burst of Titanic imagery:—

> Will all great Neptune's ocean wash this blood
> Clean from my hand? No, this my hand will rather
> The multitudinous seas incarnadine,
> Making the green one red.

Of this inner Nemesis Holinshed has but the faintest suggestion. On the other hand, the supernatural interventions which precipitate Macbeth's outer doom had been for two centuries an inseparable part of his story.[9]

---

[9] The earliest known form of the witches' prophecy is given by Wyntoun, *Orygynale Cronykil of Scotland*, vi. 18. 17 f. (c. 1424):—

> He thowcht, quhile he wes swa sythand,
> He sawe thre Wemen by gangend;

Holinshed's version employs a formidable apparatus of enchantment. Macbeth receives three warnings, on three occasions, from three distinct classes of prophetically gifted beings. Three 'fairies or weird sisters' hail him at the outset. After the death of Banquo he is warned by 'certain wizards in whose words he put great confidence (for that the prophecy had happened so right, which the three fairies or weird sisters had declared unto him) how that he ought to take heed of Macduff.' He thereupon plans Macduff's death, but desists when 'a certain witch, whom he had in great trust,' assures him that he 'should never be slain by man born of woman, nor vanquished till the wood of Birnam came to the castle of Dunsinane.' Obvious dramatic economy forbade this lavish distribution of the role of 'metaphysical aid'; and Shakespeare has blended the characteristics of all three in his weird-sister witches, who should be women 'but that their beards forbid me to interpret that they are so'; who tread the earth but seem not like its inhabitants; vanish like bubbles of the air, and speak a language which admits the extremes of sublimity and grossness,[10] of mystic suggestion and realistic detail, the wild elemental poetry of wind and storm, and the recondite lore of the foul and noisome potencies of matter. The hideous imaginings of popular and academic demonology, so busily promoted by the king, are drawn upon without reserve; but we see them through an enchanted atmosphere. It is clear that these beings, who so vitally moulded the fate of the traditional Macbeth, were not, for Shakespeare, like the dagger and the ghost, mere creations of his feverish brain, embodied symbols of his ambitious dreams. It is equally clear that for Shakespeare here, as elsewhere, the problem of fate and metaphysical influence lies in the mind of man. The witches' 'All hail!' on the blasted heath is as real for Banquo as for Macbeth, but they effect nothing with this honest and clear-headed Scot, who 'neither begs nor fears their favours nor their hate,' and is content to await the good fortune which, 'if the devil spoke true,' will come of itself without his stir. Banquo has been compared with Horatio, as the 'unimaginative, limited, but upright man of affairs,' to whom the witches and ghosts are significantly 'dumb' which 'speak' with such momentous effect to a

---

> And þai Wemen þan thowcht he
> Thre Werd Systrys mast lyk to be.
> þe first he hard say gangand by,
> Lo yhondr þe Thayne of Crombawchty.
> þe toþir Woman sayd agayne,
> Of Moraye yhondyre I se þe Thayne.
> þe pryd þan sayd, 'I se þe kyng.'
> Al þis he herd in hys dremyng.

[10] All attempts to suggest that Shakespeare distinguished, like Holinshed, between the 'weird sisters' and the 'witches' break down before the unquestionable fact that the 'witches' are repeatedly called the weird sisters (iii. 4. 133, v. 1. 136).

Hamlet and a Macbeth. The contrast between the man whose dangerously acute sensibilities invoke his tragic fate, and the sagacious man of action who is his truest ally or his deadliest foe, recurs continually in the tragedies: in Lear and Kent, Coriolanus and Menenius; in Othello and Iago, Antony and Caesar. In all of these the 'limitations' of the man of action are more salient than in Banquo, for whose ideal portraiture Shakespeare had, as we have seen, no warrant in Holinshed Macbeth, the king by foul play, is no match in 'royalty of nature' for the ancestor of kings; his genius is rebuked under him, 'as it is said Mark Antony's was by Caesar'; and the stimuli of evil suggestion which win Macbeth so lightly to his own harm, are foiled less by Banquo's want of imaginative sensibility than by his clear insight, wisdom, and valour. Macbeth's ready yielding is partly confusion of mind and partly want of nerve; Banquo's 'wisdom' would have fortified him in the thought which he grasps for one lucid moment: 'If chance will have me king, why, chance may crown me, without my stir.' Banquo's 'dauntless temper' would have held him firm when Duncan's nomination of an heir appeared to cut off all ways but 'the shortest' to the crown. Banquo reads at the outset the riddle of the unearthly intervention which Macbeth himself only divines in the last paroxysm of desperation at the close. 'To win us to our harm, the instruments of darkness tell us truths,' strikes the note of equivocation which sounds throughout the play and reaches its tragic climax in Macbeth's shrieking curse upon 'these juggling fiends...that palter with us in a double sense,'—its grotesque anticlimax in the porter's grim jest at the equivocators who knock at hell-gate since they 'could not equivocate to heaven.' The witches' cry as they sweep away into the stormlit gloom,' Fair is foul, and foul is fair,' is a fit opening formula for such a play. Even where no supernatural cunning is concerned, the style shows an unusual inclination to the Sophoclean irony of innocent phrases covering sinister depths of meaning;—as in Ross's 'And, for an earnest of a greater honour, he bade me, from him, call thee thane of Cawdor,' and Lady Macbeth's famous 'He that's coming must be provided for.' The entire atmosphere of *Macbeth*, as of no other tragedy, is oppressive with the sense of something subtly malignant as well as inexorably revengeful in the forces that rule the world; of a tragic irony in the ultimate scheme of things. But if we are permitted to read Shakespeare's "mind in the ethical atmosphere of his work, we must allow that the oppression it suggests is not despair. Macbeth is allured, not compelled, to his crime; the 'supernatural soliciting' is not a 'divine thrusting on'; he is not fate-ridden, nor irresponsible, nor the helpless sport of irresistible powers.[11] He is no symbol of the destiny of

---

[11] Cf. the strikingly-put, but I think overstated, remarks of Prof. Barrett Wendell, *W. Shakspere, p.* 305.

man; and his desperate dismissal of life as 'a tale told by an idiot, full of sound and fury, signifying nothing,' expresses only the inevitable intellectual anarchy of one who has listened to a tale full of pitfalls for the intelligence and subtle underlying meanings, and interpreted it with the naive simplicity of a child.

CHARLES HAROLD HERFORD

1903.

MACBETH

DRAMATIS PERSONAE

DUNCAN, *King of Scotland.*
MALCOLM, *his Son.*
DONALBAIN, *his Son.*
MACBETH, *General in the King's Army.*
BANQUO, *General in the King's Army.*
MACDUFF, *Nobleman of Scotland.*
LENNOX, *Nobleman of Scotland.*
ROSS, *Nobleman of Scotland.*
MENTEITH, *Nobleman of Scotland.*
ANGUS, *Nobleman of Scotland.*
CAITHNESS, *Nobleman of Scotland.*
FLEANCE, *Son to Banquo.*
SIWARD, *Earl of Northumberland, General of the English Forces.*
YOUNG SIWARD, *his Son.*
SEYTON, *an Officer attending on Macbeth.*
BOY, *Son to Macduff.*
An English Doctor. A Scotch Doctor. A Soldier. A Porter. An Old Man.

LADY MACBETH
LADY MACDUFF
Gentlewoman attending on Lady Macbeth.
HECATE, *and three Witches.*

Lords, Gentlemen, Officers, Soldiers, Murderers, Attendants, and Messengers.

The Ghost of Banquo and several other Apparitions.

SCENE: *In the end of the Fourth Act, in England; through the rest of the Play, in Scotland; and chiefly at Macbeth's Castle.*

ACT I.

SCENE I.

An Open Place.

[*Thunder and lightning. Enter three* WITCHES.]

FIRST WITCH. When shall we three meet again?
  In thunder, lightning, or in rain?
SECOND WITCH. When the hurlyburly's[1] done,
  When the battle's lost and won.
THIRD WITCH. That will be ere the set of sun.
FIRST WITCH. Where the place?
SECOND WITCH. Upon the heath.
THIRD WITCH. There to meet with Macbeth.
FIRST WITCH. I come, Graymalkin!
ALL. Paddock[2] calls.—Anon![3]
  Fair is foul, and foul is fair:[4]
  Hover through the fog and filthy air. [*Exeunt.*]

---

[1] The origin and sense of this word are given by Peacham in his *Garden of Eloquence*, 1577: "Onomatopeia, when we invent, devise, fayne, and make a name imitating the sound of that it signifyeth, as *hurlyburly*, for an *uprore* and *tumultuous stirre*." Thus also in Holinshed: "There were such *hurlie burlies* kept in every place, to the great danger of overthrowing the whole state of all government in this land."

[2] *Graymalkin* is an old name for a gray cat.—*Paddock* is *toad*; and *toadstools* were called *paddock-stools*.—In the old witchcraft lore, witches are commonly represented as having attendants called familiars, which were certain animals, such as dogs, cats, toads, rats, mice, and some others. So in *The Witch of Edmonton*, by Rowley, Dekker, and Ford, ii. 1:

> I have heard old beldams
> Talk of familiars in the shape of mice,
> Rats, ferrets, weasels, and I wot not what,
> That have appear'd, and suck'd, some say, their blood.

And in that play, mother Sawyer, the Witch, is attended by a black dog, or rather by a devil in that shape, who executes her commands. Generally, in fact, the familiar was supposed to be a devil assuming the animal's shape, and so waiting on the witch, and performing, within certain limits, whatever feats of mischief she might devise; the witch to pay his service with the final possession of her soul and body.

[3] *Anon*! was the usual answer to a call; meaning *presently* or *immediately*. Here the toad, serving as familiar, is supposed to make a signal for the Witches to leave; and *Anon*! is the reply.

[4] This is probably meant to signify the moral confusion or inversion which the Witches represent. They *love* elemental wars; and "fair is foul, and foul is fair" to them in a moral sense as well as in a physical.

SCENE II.

A Camp near Forres.

[*Alarum within. Enter* KING DUNCAN, MALCOLM, DONALBAIN,
LENNOX, *with Attendants, meeting a bleeding Soldier.*]

DUNCAN. What bloody man is that? He can report,
    As seemeth by his plight, of the revolt
    The newest state.[5]
MALCOLM. This is the sergeant,[6]
    Who, like a good and hardy soldier, fought
    'Gainst my captivity.—Hail, brave friend!
    Say to the king the knowledge of the broil
    As thou didst leave it.
SOLDIER. Doubtful it stood;
    As two spent swimmers that do cling together
    And choke their art. The merciless Macdonwald,—
    Worthy to be a rebel, for, to that,[7]
    The multiplying villainies of nature
    Do swarm upon him,—from the Western isles
    Of[8] kerns and gallowglasses is supplied;
    And fortune, on his damned quarrel[9] smiling,
    Show'd like a rebel's whore. But all's too weak;[10]
    For brave Macbeth,—well he deserves that name,—
    Disdaining fortune, with his brandish'd steel,
    Which smok'd with bloody execution,
    Like valor's minion, Carv'd out his passage

---

[5] "The *newest* state" is the *latest* condition.

[6] *Sergeants*, in ancient times, were not what are now so called; but men performing feudal military service, in rank next to esquires.

[7] To that *end*, or for that purpose; namely, to make him a rebel.

[8] *Of*, here, has the force of *with*, the two words being often used indiscriminately.— Touching the men here referred to, Holinshed has the following: "Out of Ireland in hope of the spoile came no small number of *Kernes* and *Galloglasses*, offering gladlie to serve under him, whither it should please him to lead them." Barnabe Rich thus describes them in his *New Irish Prognostication*: "The *Galloglas* succeedeth the Horseman, and he is commonly armed with a scull, a shirt of maile, and a galloglass-axe. The *Kernes* of Ireland are next in request, the very drosse and scum of the countrey, a generation of villaines not worthy to live."

[9] *Quarrel* was often used for *cause*. So in Bacon's essay *Of Marriage and Single Life*: "Wives are young men's mistresses, companions for middle age, and old men's nurses; so as a man may have a *quarrel* to marry when he will." See, also, the quotation from Holinshed in scene 4, note 69.

[10] Here, "*is* supplied" and "*is* too weak" are instances of the present with the sense of the perfect, and mixed up irregularly with preterite forms.

Till he fac'd the slave;
And ne'er shook hands,[11] nor bade farewell to him,
Till he unseam'd him from the nave to the chops,[12]
And fix'd his head upon our battlements.
DUNCAN. O valiant cousin! worthy gentleman!
SOLDIER. As whence the sun 'gins his reflection[13]
Shipwrecking storms and direful thunders break;
So from that spring, whence comfort seem'd to come
Discomfort swells. Mark, King of Scotland, mark:
No sooner justice had, with valor arm'd,
Compell'd these skipping kerns to trust their heels,
But the Norweyan lord, surveying vantage,
With furbish'd arms[14] and new supplies of men,
Began a fresh assault.
DUNCAN. Dismay'd not this
Our captains,[15] Macbeth and Banquo?
SOLDIER. Yes;
As sparrows eagles, or the hare the lion.
If I say sooth, I must report they were
As cannons overcharg'd with double cracks;[16]
So they
Doubly redoubled strokes upon the foe:
Except they meant to bathe in reeking wounds,
Or memorize[17] another Golgotha,
I cannot tell:—
But I am faint; my gashes cry for help.
DUNCAN. So well thy words become thee as thy wounds;
They smack of honour both.—Go, get him surgeons.

---

[11] To *shake hands with* a thing, as the phrase was formerly used, is to *take leave of it.* So Sir Thomas Browne, in his *Religio Medici,* 1643: "I have *shaken hands with delight* in my warm blood and canicular days; I perceive I do anticipate the vices of age;" &c.

[12] *Nave* for *navel,* probably. Such a sword-stroke upwards seems rather odd, but queer things have often happened in mortal combats. So in Nash's *Dido, Queen of Carthage,* 1594: "Then from the *navel* to the *throat* at once he ript old Priam." Also in Shadwell's *Libertine,* 1676: "I will rip you from the *navel* to the *chin.*"

[13] *Reflection* is here put, apparently, for *radiance* or *light.* So that the place "whence the Sun gives his reflection" is the heavens or the sky.

[14] That is, arms gleaming with unstained *brightness; fresh.*—Surveying *vantage* is *watching* his *opportunity.*

[15] Here *captains* was probably meant to be a trisyllable, as if it were spelt *capitains.* We have the word used repeatedly so.

[16] *Overcharged* with double *cracks* is, as we should say, *loaded* with double *charges; crack* being put for that which makes the crack.

[17] To *memorize* is to *make famous* or *memorable. Except* is here equivalent to *unless.* "Unless they meant to make the spot as famous as Golgotha, I cannot tell *what they meant.*"

[*Exit Soldier, attended.*]

Who comes here?
MALCOLM. The worthy Thane of Ross.
LENNOX. What haste[18] looks through his eyes! So should he look
  That seems[19] to speak things strange.

[*Enter* ROSS.]

ROSS. God save the King!
DUNCAN. Whence cam'st thou, worthy thane?
ROSS. From Fife, great king;
  Where the Norweyan banners flout the sky
  And fan our people cold.[20] Norway himself,
  With terrible numbers,
  Assisted by that most disloyal traitor,
  The Thane of Cawdor, began a dismal conflict;
  Till that Bellona's bridegroom, lapp'd in proof,[21]
  Confronted him with self caparisons,[22]
  Point against point rebellious, arm 'gainst arm,
  Curbing his lavish spirit:[23] and, to conclude,
  The victory fell on us.
DUNCAN. Great happiness!
ROSS. —that[24] now
  Sweno, the Norways' king, craves composition;
· Nor would we deign him burial of his men
  Till he disbursed, at Saint Colme's-inch,[25]

---

[18] We should say, "What *a* haste."

[19] It appears that to *seem* was sometimes used with the exact sense of to *will* or to *mean*. So, afterwards, in scene 5: "Which fate and metaphysical aid doth *seem* to have thee crown'd withal."

[20] "The banners, proudly reared aloft and fluttering in the wind, seemed to mock or insult the sky,—'laughing banners'; while the sight of them struck chills of dread and dismay into our men." *Flout* and *fan* for *flouted* and *fanned*; instances of what is called "the historic present." See note 10.

[21] "Lapp'd in proof" is covered with impenetrable armour, or "armour of proof," as it is called.—Bellona was the old Roman goddess of war; the companion and, as some thought, the sister of Mars. Steevens laughed at the Poet's ignorance in making her the wife of Mars; whereas he plainly makes her the bride of Macbeth.

[22] *Caparisons* for *arms*, offensive and defensive; the trappings and furniture of personal fighting. Here, as often, *self* is equivalent to *self-same*. So that the meaning is, Macbeth confronted the rebel Cawdor with just such arms as Cawdor himself had. It was Scot against Scot.

[23] That is, checking or repressing his *reckless* or *prodigal daring*.

[24] *That* was continually used with the force of *so that*, or *insomuch that.*— *Composition* for *armistice* or *terms of peace*; as in the phrase to *compound a quarrel*.

[25] *Colme's* is here a dissyllable. *Colme's Inch*, now called *Inchcomb*, is a small island, lying in the Firth of Edinburgh, with an abbey upon it dedicated to St. Columb.

Ten thousand dollars to our general use.
DUNCAN. No more that Thane of Cawdor shall deceive
  Our bosom interest:—go pronounce his present death,
  And with his former title greet Macbeth.
ROSS. I'll see it done.
DUNCAN. What he hath lost, noble Macbeth hath won. [*Exeunt.*]

SCENE III.

A Heath.

[*Thunder. Enter the three* WITCHES.]

FIRST WITCH. Where hast thou been, sister?
SECOND WITCH. Killing swine.
THIRD WITCH. Sister, where thou?
FIRST WITCH. A sailor's wife had chestnuts in her lap,
  And mounch'd, and mounch'd, and mounch'd: "Give me," quoth I:
  "Aroint thee,[26] witch!" the rump-fed ronyon[27] cries.
  Her husband's to Aleppo gone, master o' the *Tiger*:
  But in a sieve I'll thither sail,
  And, like a rat without a tail,[28]
  I'll do, I'll do, and I'll do.[29]
SECOND WITCH. I'll give thee a wind.
FIRST WITCH. Thou art kind.[30]
THIRD WITCH. And I another.
FIRST WITCH. I myself have all the other:
  And the very ports they blow,
  All the quarters that they know

Inch or *inse*, in Erse, signifies an island.

[26] *Aroint thee*! is an old exorcism against witches; meaning, apparently, *away*! *stand off*! or be *gone*! The etymology of the word is uncertain.

[27] *Ronyon* is said to be from *ronger*, French, which signifies to *gnaw* or *corrode*. It thus carries the sense of *scurvy* or *mangy*.—*Rump-fed* is, probably, fed on broken meats or the refuse of wealthy tables. Some, however, take it to mean pampered; fed on the best pieces.

[28] Scot, in his *Discovery of Witchcraft*, 1584, says it was believed that witches "could sail in an egg-shell, a cockle or muscle-shell through and under the tempestuous seas." And in the *Life of Doctor Fian, a notable Sorcerer*: "All they together went to sea, each one in a riddle or cive, and went in the same very substantially, with flaggons of wine making merrie, and drinking by the way in the same riddles or cives."—It was the belief of the times that, though a witch could assume the form of any animal she pleased, the *tail* would still be wanting.

[29] *I'll do* is a threat of gnawing a hole through the hull of the ship so as to make her spring a-leak.

[30] This free gift of a wind is to be taken as an act of sisterly kindness; witches being thought to have the power of *selling* winds.

I' the shipman's card.[31]
I will drain him dry as hay:
Sleep shall neither night nor day
Hang upon his pent-house lid;[32]
He shall live a man forbid:[33]
Weary seven-nights nine times nine
Shall he dwindle, peak, and pine:[34]
Though his bark cannot be lost,
Yet it shall be tempest-tost.—
Look what I have.
SECOND WITCH. Show me, show me.
FIRST WITCH. Here I have a pilot's thumb,
Wreck'd as homeward he did come.

[*Drum within.*]

THIRD WITCH. A drum, a drum!
Macbeth doth come.
ALL. The Weird Sisters,[35] hand in hand,
Posters[36] of the sea and land,
Thus do go about, about:
Thrice to thine, and thrice to mine,
And thrice again, to make up nine.[37]
Peace!—the charm's wound up.

---

[31] The seaman's *chart*, which shows all the points of the compass, as we call them, marked down in the radii of a circle.

[32] "Penthouse lid" is eyelid protected as by a penthouse roof. So in Drayton's *David and Goliath*: "His brows like two steep *penthouses* hung down over his *eyelids*."

[33] To live *forbid* is to live *under a curse or an interdict*; pursued by an evil fate.— *Sev'n-night* is *a week*.

[34] To *peak* is to *grow thin*. This was supposed to be wrought by means of a waxen figure. Holinshed, describing the means used for destroying King Duff, says that the witches were found roasting an image of him before the fire; and that, as the image wasted, the King's body broke forth in sweat, while the words of enchantment kept him from sleep.

[35] *Weird* is from the Saxon *wyrd*, and means the same as the Latin *fatum*; so that *weird sisters* is the *fatal sisters*, or the *sisters of fate*. Gawin Douglas, in his translation of Virgil, renders *Parcœ* by *weird sisters*. Which agrees well with Holinshed in the passage which the Poet no doubt had in his eye: "The common opinion was, that these women were either the *weird sisters*, that is (as ye would say) the *goddesses of destinie*, or else some nymphs or feiries, indued with knowledge of prophesie by their necromanticall science, bicause everie thing came to passe as they had spoken."

[36] *Posters* is *rapid travelers*; going with a postman's speed.

[37] Here the Witches perform a sort of incantation by joining hands, and dancing round in a ring, three rounds for each. Odd numbers and multiples of odd numbers, especially three and nine, were thought to have great magical power in thus winding up a charm.

[*Enter* MACBETH *and* BANQUO.]

MACBETH. So foul and fair a day[38] I have not seen.
BANQUO. How far is't call'd to Forres?—What are these
    So wither'd, and so wild in their attire,
    That look not like the inhabitants o' the earth,
    And yet are on't?—Live you? or are you aught
    That man may question? You seem to understand me,
    By each at once her chappy finger laying
    Upon her skinny lips:—you should be women,
    And yet your beards forbid me to interpret
    That you are so.
MACBETH. Speak, if you can;—what are you?
FIRST WITCH. All hail, Macbeth! hail to thee, Thane of Glamis!
SECOND WITCH. All hail, Macbeth! hail to thee, Thane of Cawdor!
THIRD WITCH. All hail, Macbeth! that shalt be king hereafter!
BANQUO. Good sir, why do you start; and seem to fear
    Things that do sound so fair?—I' the name of truth,
    Are ye fantastical,[39] or that indeed
    Which outwardly ye show? My noble partner
    You greet with present grace and great prediction
    Of noble having and of royal hope,[40]
    That he seems rapt withal:—to me you speak not:
    If you can look into the seeds of time,
    And say which grain will grow, and which will not,
    Speak then to me, who neither beg nor fear
    Your favours nor your hate.
FIRST WITCH. Hail!
SECOND WITCH. Hail!
THIRD WITCH. Hail!
FIRST WITCH. Lesser than Macbeth, and greater.
SECOND WITCH. Not so happy, yet much happier.
THIRD WITCH. Thou shalt get kings, though thou be none:
    So all hail, Macbeth and Banquo!
FIRST WITCH. Banquo and Macbeth, all hail!
MACBETH. Stay, you imperfect speakers, tell me more:
    By Sinel's death I know I am Thane of Glamis;[41]

---

[38] A day fouled with storm, but brightened with victory.

[39] That is, "Are ye imaginary beings, creatures of *fantasy*?"

[40] Here, again, *that* has the force of *so that*.—*Present grace* refers to *noble having*, and *great prediction* to *royal hope*; and the Poet often uses *having* for *possession*. A similar distribution of terms occurs a little after: "Who neither beg nor fear your favours nor your hate."

[41] Macbeth was the son of Sinel, Thane of Glamis, so that this title was rightfully his by inheritance.

But how of Cawdor? The Thane of Cawdor lives,
A prosperous gentleman;[42] and to be king
Stands not within the prospect of belief,
No more than to be Cawdor. Say from whence
You owe[43] this strange intelligence? or why
Upon this blasted heath you stop our way
With such prophetic greeting? Speak, I charge you.

[WITCHES *vanish.*]

BANQUO. The earth hath bubbles, as the water has,
  And these are of them:——whither are they vanish'd?
MACBETH. Into the air; and what seem'd corporal melted
  As breath into the wind.——Would they had stay'd!
BANQUO. Were such things here as we do speak about?
  Or have we eaten on the insane root[44]
  That takes the reason prisoner?
MACBETH. Your children shall be kings.
BANQUO. You shall be king.
MACBETH. And Thane of Cawdor too; went it not so?
BANQUO. To the selfsame tune and words. Who's here?

[*Enter* ROSS *and* ANGUS.]

ROSS. The king hath happily receiv'd, Macbeth,
  The news of thy success: and when he reads
  Thy personal venture in the rebels' fight,
  His wonders and his praises do contend
  What should be thine or his:[45] silenc'd with that,

---

[42] We have a strange discrepancy here. In the preceding scene, Macbeth is said to have met Cawdor face to face in the ranks of Norway: he must therefore have known him to be a rebel and traitor; yet he here describes him in terms quite inconsistent with such knowledge.

[43] To *owe* for to *own*, to *have*, to *possess*, occurs continually.

[44] "The insane root" is *henbane* or *hemlock*. So in Batman's *Commentary on Bartholome de Proprietate Rerum*: "Henbane is called *insana*, mad, for the use thereof is perillous; for if it be eate or dronke it breedeth madnesse, or slow lykenesse of sleepe. Therefore this hearb is commonly called mirilidium, for it taketh away wit and reason." And in Greene's *Never too Late*: "You have gazed against the sun, and so blemished your sight, or else you have eaten of the roots of *hemlock*, that makes men's eyes conceit unseen objects."——*On* and *of* were used indifferently in such cases.

[45] The meaning probably is, "His wonders and his praises are so earnest and enthusiastic, that they seem to be debating or raising the question whether what is his ought not to be thine,——whether you ought not to be in his place." Such a thought, or *seeming* thought, on the King's part, would naturally act upon Macbeth as a further spur to his ambition. But that is a thought which the King cannot breathe aloud; it would be a sort of treason to the State and to himself; he is *silenced* by it.

In viewing o'er the rest o' the self-same day,
He finds thee in the stout Norweyan ranks,
Nothing afeard of what thyself didst make,[46]
Strange images of death. As thick as hail
Came post with post;[47] and every one did bear
Thy praises in his kingdom's great defense,
And pour'd them down before him.

ANGUS. We are sent
To give thee, from our royal master, thanks;
Only to herald thee into his sight,
Not pay thee.

ROSS. And, for an earnest of a greater honour,
He bade me, from him, call thee Thane of Cawdor:
In which addition,[48] hail, most worthy thane,
For it is thine.

BANQUO. [*Aside.*] What, can the Devil speak true?

MACBETH. The Thane of Cawdor lives: why do you dress me
In borrow'd robes?

ANGUS. Who was the Thane lives yet;
But under heavy judgement bears that life
Which he deserves to lose. Whether he was combin'd
With those of Norway, or did line[49] the rebel
With hidden help and vantage, or that with both
He labour'd in his country's wreck, I know not;
But treasons capital, confess'd and proved,
Have overthrown him.

MACBETH. [*Aside.*] Glamis, and Thane of Cawdor:
The greatest is behind.—[*To* ROSS *and* ANGUS.] Thanks for your
pains.—
[*Aside to* BANQUO.] Do you not hope your children shall be
kings,
When those that gave the *Thane of Cawdor* to me
Promis'd no less to them?

BANQUO. [*Aside to* MACBETH.] That, trusted home,[50]
Might yet enkindle you unto the crown,
Besides the Thane of Cawdor. But 'tis strange:

---

[46] That is, "*not at all* afraid of the death which you were dealing upon the enemy." The Poet often uses *nothing* thus as a strong negative.

[47] Meaning, "messengers came as *fast* as one can *count*." The use of *thick* for *fast* occurs repeatedly. So we have *speaks thick* used of one who talks so fast that his words tread on each other's heels.—The Poet often has to *tell* also for to *count*. And we still say "keep *tally*" for "keep *count*." So Milton in *L'Allegro*. "And every shepherd *tells* his *tale*"; that is, *counts* the *number* of his sheep, or to see whether the number is full.

[48] Here, as often, *addition* is *title*, mark of *distinction*.

[49] To *line*, here, is to *strengthen*. Often so.

[50] *Home* is *thoroughly* or *to the uttermost*.

And oftentimes to win us to our harm,
The instruments of darkness tell us truths;
Win us with honest trifles, to betray's[51]
In deepest consequence.—
Cousins, a word, I pray you.
MACBETH. [*Aside.*] Two truths are told,
As happy prologues to the swelling act
Of the imperial theme.[52]—I thank you, gentlemen.—
[*Aside.*] This supernatural soliciting
Cannot be ill; cannot be good:—if ill,
Why hath it given me earnest of success,
Commencing in a truth? I am Thane of Cawdor:
If good, why do I yield to that suggestion[53]
Whose horrid image doth unfix my hair,
And make my seated heart knock at my ribs,
Against the use of nature? Present fears[54]
Are less than horrible imaginings:
My thought, whose murder yet is but fantastical,
Shakes so my single state of man,[55] that function
Is smother'd in surmise; and nothing is
But what is not.[56]
BANQUO. Look, how our partner's rapt.
MACBETH. [*Aside.*] If chance will have me king, why, chance may
crown me

---

[51] *Betray's* for *betray us*. The Poet has many such contractions.—It is nowise likely that Shakespeare was a reader of Livy; yet we have here a striking resemblance to a passage in that author, Book xxviii. 42, 4: "An Syphaci Numidisque credis? satis sit semel creditum: non semper temeritas est felix, et *fraus fidem in parvis sibi præstruit ut, quum operæ pretium sit, cum mercede magna fallat.*"

[52] *Happy* is *auspicious*, like the Latin *felix*; *swelling* is *grand, imposing*; and *act* is *drama.* Thus the image is of the stage, with an august drama of kingly state to be performed; the inspiring prologue has been spoken, and the glorious action is about to commence.

[53] The use of *suggestion* for *temptation* was common.—Macbeth construes the "prophetic greeting" into an instigation to murder, and accepts it as such, though while doing so he shudders at the conception.

[54] *Fears* for *objects* of fear, *dangers* or *terrors*; the effect for the cause.

[55] "My thought, though it is only of a murder in imagination or fantasy, so disturbs my feeble manhood of reason." The Poet repeatedly uses *single* thus for *weak* or *feeble.*

[56] That is, *facts* are lost sight of; he *sees* nothing but what is unreal, nothing but the spectres of his own fancy. So, likewise, in the preceding clause: the mind is crippled, disabled for its proper function or office by the apprehensions and surmises that throng upon him. Macbeth's conscience here acts through his imagination, sets it all on fire; and he is terror-stricken, and lost to the things before him, as the elements of evil within him gather and fashion themselves into the wicked purpose. Of this wonderful development of character Coleridge justly says: "So surely is the guilt in its germ anterior to the supposed cause and immediate temptation." And again: "Every word of his soliloquy shows the early birth-date of his guilt. He wishes the end, but is irresolute as to the means; conscience distinctly warns him, and he lulls it imperfectly."

Without my stir.
BANQUO. New honours come upon him,
    Like our strange garments, cleave not to their mould
    But with the aid of use.
MACBETH. [*Aside.*] Come what come may,
    Time and the hour[57] runs through the roughest day.
BANQUO. Worthy Macbeth, we stay upon your leisure.[58]
MACBETH. Give me your favour:—my dull brain was wrought
    With things forgotten.[59] Kind gentlemen, your pains
    Are register'd where every day I turn
    The leaf to read them.[60] Let us toward the king.—
    [*Aside to* BANQUO.] Think upon what hath chanc'd; and, at more
        time,
    The interim having weigh'd it, let us speak
    Our free hearts[61] each to other.
BANQUO. [*Aside to* MACBETH.] Very gladly.
MACBETH. [*Aside to* BANQUO.] Till then, enough.—Come, friends.
    [*Exeunt.*]

SCENE IV.

Forres. A Room in the Palace.

[*Flourish. Enter* DUNCAN, MALCOLM,
DONALBAIN, LENNOX, *and Attendants.*]

DUNCAN. Is execution done on Cawdor? Are not
    Those in commission yet return'd?
MALCOLM. My liege,
    They are not yet come back. But I have spoke
    With one that saw him die: who did report,
    That very frankly he confess'd his treasons;
    Implor'd your highness' pardon; and set forth
    A deep repentance: nothing in his life
    Became him like the leaving it; he died

---

[57] "Time and the hour" is an old reduplicate phrase occurring repeatedly in the writers of Shakespeare's time. The Italians have one just like it,—*il tempo e l'ore*. The sense of the passage is well explained by Heath: "The advantage of time and of seizing the favourable hour, whenever it shall present itself, will enable me to make my way through all obstruction and opposition. Every one knows the Spanish proverb,—'Time and I against any two.'"

[58] "Stay *upon* your leisure" is stay *for* or *await* your leisure.

[59] "Was exercised or absorbed in trying to recall forgotten things." A pretext put forth to hide the true cause of his trance of guilty thought.

[60] He means that he has noted them down on the tablets of his memory.

[61] "Speak our *free* hearts" is speak our hearts *freely.*

As one that had been studied in his death[62]
To throw away the dearest thing he ow'd
As 'twere a careless trifle.[63]
DUNCAN. There's no art
To find the mind's construction in the face:
He was a gentleman on whom I built
An absolute trust.—

[*Enter* MACBETH, BANQUO, ROSS, *and* ANGUS.]

O worthiest cousin!
The sin of my ingratitude even now
Was heavy on me: thou art so far before,
That swiftest wing of recompense is slow
To overtake thee.[64] Would thou hadst less deserv'd;
That the proportion both of thanks and payment
Might have been mine![65] only I have left to say,
More is thy due than more than all can pay.
MACBETH. The service and the loyalty I owe,
In doing it, pays itself. Your highness' part
Is to receive our duties: and our duties
Are to your throne and state, children and servants;[66]
Which do but what they should, by doing everything
Safe toward your love and honour.[67]
DUNCAN. Welcome hither:
I have begun to plant thee, and will labor
To make thee full of growing.—Noble Banquo,
That hast no less deserv'd, nor must be known
No less to have done so, let me infold thee
And hold thee to my heart.
BANQUO. There if I grow,
The harvest is your own.
DUNCAN. My plenteous joys,

---

[62] That is, well instructed in the art of dying.

[63] Meaning a trifle *not worth caring for. As* for *as if.* Often so.

[64] The meaning is, "*too* slow to overtake thee."

[65] "That my return of thanks and payment might have been *proportionable* to thy deserts, or in due proportion with them."

[66] *Duties* is here put, apparently, for the faculties and labours of duty; the meaning being, "All our works and forces of duty are children and servants to your throne and state." Hypocrisy and hyperbole are apt to go together; and so here Macbeth overacts the part of loyalty, and tries how high he can strain up his expression of it.

[67] I am not quite clear whether this means "With a firm and *sure* purpose to have you loved and honoured," or, "So as to merit and *secure* love and honour from you." Perhaps both; as the Poet is fond of condensing two or more meanings into one expression.

Wanton in fulness, seek to hide themselves
In drops of sorrow.[68]—Sons, kinsmen, thanes,
And you whose places are the nearest, know,
We will establish our estate upon
Our eldest, Malcolm; whom we name hereafter
The Prince of Cumberland:[69] which honour must
Not unaccompanied invest him only,
But signs of nobleness, like stars, shall shine
On all deservers.—From hence to Inverness,
And bind us further to you.

MACBETH. The rest is labor, which[70] is not used for you:
I'll be myself the harbinger, and make joyful
The hearing of my wife with your approach;
So, humbly take my leave.

DUNCAN. My worthy Cawdor!

MACBETH. [*Aside.*] The Prince of Cumberland! that is a step,
On which I must fall down, or else o'erleap,
For in my way it lies. Stars, hide your fires;[71]
Let not light see my black and deep desires:
The eye wink[72] at the hand! yet let that be,
Which the eye fears, when it is done, to see. [*Exit.*]

DUNCAN. True, worthy Banquo;[73] he is full so valiant;
And in his commendations I am fed,—
It is a banquet to me. Let us after him,
Whose care is gone before to bid us welcome:
It is a peerless kinsman. [*Flourish. Exeunt.*]

---

[68] The gentle and amiable sovereign means that his joys swell up so high as to overflow in tears. The Poet has several like expressions.

[69] So in Holinshed: "Duncan, having two sons, made the elder of them, called Malcolm, Prince of Cumberland, as it was thereby to appoint him his successor in his kingdome immediatelie after his decease. Macbeth sorely troubled herewith, for that he saw by this means his hope sore hindered, began to take counsel how he might usurpe the kingdome by force, having a just *quarrel* so to due, (as he tooke the matter,) for that Duncane did what in him lay to defraud him of all manner of title and claime, which he might in time to come pretend, unto the crowne." Cumberland was then held in fief of the English crown.

[70] *Which* refers to *rest*, not to *labour*. "Even the repose, which is not taken for your sake, is a labour to me."

[71] We are not to understand from this that the present scene takes place in the night. Macbeth is contemplating night as the time when the murder is to be done, and his appeal to the stars has reference to that.

[72] "*Let* the eye wink" is the meaning. *Wink at* is *encourage* or *prompt*.

[73] During Macbeth's last speech Duncan and Banquo were conversing apart, he being the subject of their talk. The beginning of Duncan's speech refers to something Banquo has said in praise of Macbeth.

Inverness. A Room in MACBETH'*s Castle.*

[*Enter* LADY MACBETH, *reading a letter.*]

LADY MACBETH. [*Reads.*] "They met me in the day of success; and
I have learned by the perfectest report they have more in them than
mortal knowledge. When I burned in desire to question them
further, they made themselves air, into which they vanished.
Whiles I stood rapt in the wonder of it, came missives[74] from the
king, who all-hailed me, 'Thane of Cawdor'; by which title, before,
these weird sisters saluted me, and referred me to the coming on of
time, with 'Hail, king that shalt be!' This have I thought good to
deliver thee, my dearest partner of greatness; that thou mightst not
lose the dues of rejoicing, by being ignorant of what greatness is
promised thee. Lay it to thy heart, and farewell."

Glamis thou art, and Cawdor; and shalt be
What thou art promis'd; yet do I fear thy nature;
It is too full o' the milk of human kindness
To catch the nearest way: thou wouldst be great;
Art not without ambition; but without
The illness[75] should attend it. What thou wouldst highly,
That wouldst thou holily; wouldst not play false,
And yet wouldst wrongly win: thou'dst have, great Glamis,
That which cries, *Thus thou must do,*[76] if thou have it:
And that which rather thou dost fear to do
Than wishest should be undone. Hie thee hither,
That I may pour my spirits in thine ear;
And chastise with the valor of my tongue
All that impedes thee from the golden round,
Which fate and metaphysical[77] aid doth seem

---

[74] *Missives* for *messengers.* So in *Antony and Cleopatra,* ii. 2: "And with taunts did
gibe my *missive* out of audience."

[75] *Illness* in the sense, not only of *wickedness,* but of remorselessness or *hardness of
heart.*—"Macbeth," says Coleridge, "is described by Lady Macbeth so as at the same
time to reveal her own character. Could he have every thing he wanted, he would rather
have it innocently; ignorant, as, alas, how many of us are! that he who wishes a temporal
end for itself does in truth will the means; and hence the danger of indulging fancies."

[76] Editors differ as to how much is here uttered by the voice which Lady Macbeth
imagines speaking to her husband.

[77] *Metaphysical* for *supernatural.* So in Florio's *World of Words,* 1598: "Metafisico,
one that professeth things supernaturall." And in Minsheu's *Spanish Dictionary,* 1599:
"Metafisica, things supernaturall, metaphisickes."—For this use of *seem,* see page 26,

To have thee crown'd withal.—

[*Enter an* ATTENDANT.]

What is your tidings?
ATTENDANT. The king comes here tonight.
LADY MACBETH. Thou'rt mad to say it:
    Is not thy master with him? who, were't so,
    Would have inform'd for preparation.
ATTENDANT. So please you, it is true: Our thane is coming:
    One of my fellows had the speed of him;
    Who, almost dead for breath, had scarcely more
    Than would make up his message.
LADY MACBETH. Give him tending;
    He brings great news.—[*Exit Attendant.*]
        The raven himself is hoarse
    That croaks the fatal entrance[78] of Duncan
    Under my battlements. Come, you spirits
    That tend on mortal[79] thoughts, unsex me here;
    And fill me, from the crown to the toe, top-full
    Of direst cruelty! make thick my blood,
    Stop up the access and passage to remorse,[80]
    That no compunctious visitings of nature
    Shake my fell purpose, nor keep peace between
    The effect and it![81] Come to my woman's breasts,
    And take my milk for gall,[82] your murdering ministers,
    Wherever in your sightless substances
    You wait on nature's mischief! Come, thick night,
    And pall thee[83] in the dunnest smoke of hell

---

note 19.

[78] Meaning, probably, the raven *has made himself hoarse with croaking*, or has croaked so loud and long as to become hoarse, over the fatal entrance, &c. The figure of speech called *prolepsis*. Shakespeare has other allusions to the ominousness of the raven's croak; as he also has many such *anticipative* expressions.

[79] *Mortal* and *deadly* were synonymous in Shakespeare's time. Later in this play we have "the *mortal* sword," and "*mortal* gashes."—The spirits here addressed are thus described in Nashe's *Pierce Pennilesse*: "The second kind of devils, which he most employeth, are those northern *Martii*, called the *spirits of revenge*, and the authors of massacres, and seedsmen of mischief; for they have commission to incense men to rapines, sacrilege, theft, murder, wrath, fury, and all manner of cruelties."

[80] *Remorse* here means *pity*, the relentings of compassion; as it generally does in the writings of Shakespeare's time.

[81] Peace is of course *broken* between the effect and the purpose when the two stand in conflict or at odds with each other; that is, when the purpose remains unexecuted.

[82] "Take away my milk, and give me gall instead," is probably the meaning. In her fiery thirst of power, Lady Macbeth feels that her woman's heart is unequal to the calls of her ambition, and she would fain exchange her "milk of human kindness," for a fiercer infusion.

That my keen knife see not the wound it makes
Nor heaven peep through the blanket of the dark,[84]
To cry, *Hold, hold*!

[*Enter* MACBETH.]

    Great Glamis! Worthy Cawdor!
Greater than both, by the all-hail hereafter!
Thy letters have transported me beyond
This ignorant present, and I feel now
The future in the instant.[85]
MACBETH. My dearest love,
Duncan comes here tonight.
LADY MACBETH. And when goes hence?
MACBETH. To-morrow,—as he purposes.
LADY MACBETH. O, never
Shall sun that morrow see!
Your face, my thane, is as a book where men
May read strange matters:—to beguile the time,
Look like the time;[86] bear welcome in your eye,
Your hand, your tongue: look like the innocent flower,
But be the serpent under't. He that's coming
Must be provided for: and you shall put
This night's great business into my dispatch;
Which shall to all our nights and days to come
Give solely sovereign sway and masterdom.
MACBETH. We will speak further.
LADY MACBETH. Only look up clear;
To alter favour[87] ever is to fear:

---

[83] "*Thick* night" is explained by "light *thickens*," later in the play. We still have the phrase "*thick* darkness."—To *pall* is to *robe*, to *shroud*, to *wrap*: from the Latin *pallium*, a *cloak* or *mantle*.

[84] The metaphor of darkness being a blanket wrapped round the world, so as to keep the Divine Eye from seeing what Lady Macbeth longs and expects to have done, is just such a one as it was fitting for the boldest of poets to put into the mouth of the boldest of women. The old poets, however, were rather fond of representing night in some such way. So in *The Faerie Queene*, i. 4, 44: "Now whenas darksome night had all displayd her coleblacke *curtein* over brightest skye." And in Milton's *Ode on the Passion*: "Befriend me, night; over the pole thy thickest *mantle* throw."

[85] *Instant* in the Latin sense of *instans*; that which is pressing. The enthusiasm of her newly-kindled expectation quickens the dull present with the spirit of the future, and gives to hope the life and substance of fruition.

[86] *Time* is here put for its contents, or what occurs in time. It is a time of full-hearted welcome and hospitality; and such are the looks which Macbeth is urged to counterfeit.

[87] *Favour* is *countenance*.—Lady Macbeth is here mad, or inspired, with a. kind of extemporized ferocity, so that she feels herself able to perform without flinching the crime she has conceived, if her husband will only keep his face from telling any tales of their purpose.

Leave all the rest to me. [*Exeunt.*]

SCENE VI.

The Same. Before MACBETH'*s Castle.*

[*Hautboys and torches. Enter* DUNCAN, MALCOLM,
DONALBAIN, BANQUO, LENNOX, MACDUFF, ROSS,
ANGUS, *and* ATTENDANTS.]

DUNCAN. This castle hath a pleasant seat: the air
    Nimbly and sweetly recommends itself
    Unto our gentle senses.[88]
BANQUO. This guest of summer,
    The temple-haunting martlet, does approve,[89]
    By his lov'd mansionry, that the heaven's breath
    Smells wooingly here: no jutty, frieze,
    Buttress, nor coign of vantage,[90] but this bird hath made
    His pendant bed and procreant cradle:
    Where they most breed and haunt, I have observ'd
    The air is delicate.[91]

[*Enter* LADY MACBETH.]

DUNCAN. See, see, our honour'd hostess!—
    The love that follows us sometime[92] is our trouble,
    Which still we thank as love. Herein I teach you
    How you shall bid God 'ield us[93] for your pains,
    And thank us for your trouble.
LADY MACBETH. All our service

---

[88] That is, "The air, by its purity and sweetness, attempers our senses to its own state, and so *makes* them gentle, or sweetens them into gentleness." Another proleptical form of speech. See page 37, note 78.

[89] *Approve* in the sense of *prove* simply, or *make evident.*

[90] "Coigne of vantage "is a convenient nook or corner; *coigne* being a corner-stone at the exterior angle of a building. So in *Coriolanus,* v. 4: "See you yond coigne o' the Capital, yond corner-stone?"

[91] The subject of this quiet and easy conversation gives that repose so necessary to the mind after the tumultuous bustle of the preceding scenes, and perfectly contrasts the scene of horror that succeeds. This also is frequently the practice of Homer, who, from the midst of battles and horrors, relieves and refreshes the mind of the reader, by introducing some quiet rural image or picture of familiar domestic life.—REYNOLDS.

[92] *Sometime* and *sometimes* were used indiscriminately.

[93] "God *yield* us," that is, *reward* us.—To *bid* is here used in its old sense of to *pray.* So to *bid* the beads is to pray through the rosary.—The kind-hearted monarch means that his love is what puts him upon troubling them thus, and therefore they will be grateful for the pains he causes them.

In every point twice done, and then done double,
Were poor and single[94] business to contend
Against[95] those honours deep and broad wherewith
Your majesty loads our house: for those of old,
And the late dignities heap'd up to[96] them,
We rest your hermits.[97]

DUNCAN. Where's the Thane of Cawdor?
We cours'd him at the heels, and had a purpose
To be his purveyor:[98] but he rides well;
And his great love, sharp as his spur, hath holp[99] him
To his home before us. Fair and noble hostess,
We are your guest tonight.

LADY MACBETH. Your servants ever
Have theirs, themselves, and what is theirs, in compt,[100]
To make their audit at your highness' pleasure,
Still to return your own.

DUNCAN. Give me your hand; [*Taking her hand.*]
Conduct me to mine host: we love him highly,
And shall continue our graces towards him.
By your leave, hostess.[101] [*Exeunt.*]

SCENE VII.

The same. A Lobby in the Castle.

[*Hautboys and torches. Enter, and pass over, a* Sewer,[102] *and divers,*
SERVANTS *with dishes and service. Then enter* MACBETH.]

MACBETH. If it were done when 'tis done, then 'twere well
It were done quickly:[103] If the assassination

---

[94] Here, again, *too* is understood before *poor. Single*, again, also, in the sense of *weak* or *small*. See page 32, note 55, and page 34, note 64.

[95] "To contend against" here means to *vie with*, to *counterpoise* or *match*.

[96] Here, as often, *to* has the force of *in addition to*.

[97] That is, "We *remain* as hermits or *beadsmen* to pray for you."

[98] *Purveyor* is, properly, one sent before, to provide food and drink for some person or party that is to follow.

[99] *Holp* is the old preterite of *help*. So in The Psalter, generally.

[100] "*Theirs*, and *what is* theirs," means their *kindred and dependants*, and *whatever* belongs to them *as property.—In compt* is ready to answer, subject to account or reckoning. So in *Othello*, v. 2: "When we shall meet *at compt*, this look of thine will hurl my soul from Heaven, and fiends will snatch at it"; *at compt* for the clay of reckoning, or the Judgment-Day.

[101] "By your leave" is probably meant as a respectful prologue to a kiss.

[102] An officer so called from his placing the dishes on the table. From the French *essayeur*, used of one who tasted each dish to show that there was no poison in the food.

[103] "If *all* were done when the murder is done, or if the mere doing of the deed were

Could trammel up the consequence, and catch,
With his surcease, success;[104] that but this blow
Might be the be-all and the end-all—here,
But here, upon this bank and shoal of time,—
We'd jump[105] the life to come. But in these cases
We still have judgement here; that[106] we but teach
Bloody instructions, which being taught, return
To plague the inventor: this even-handed justice
Commends the ingredients of our poison'd chalice
To our own lips. He's here in double trust:
First, as I am his kinsman and his subject,
Strong both against the deed: then, as his host,
Who should against his murderer shut the door,
Not bear the knife myself. Besides, this Duncan
Hath borne his faculties[107] so meek, hath been
So clear in his great office, that his virtues
Will plead like angels, trumpet-tongued, against
The deep damnation of his taking-off:
And pity, like a naked new-born babe,
Striding the blast, or heaven's cherubin, hors'd
Upon the sightless couriers[108] of the air,
Shall blow the horrid deed in every eye,
That tears shall drown the wind.—I have no spur
To prick the sides of my intent, but only
Vaulting ambition, which o'erleaps itself,[109]
And falls on the other.

[*Enter* LADY MACBETH.]

---

sure to finish the matter, then the quicker, the better."

[104] That is, if the assassination could foreclose or shut off all sequent issues, and end with itself. *His* for *its*, referring to *assassination.*—To *trammel up* is to *entangle* as in a net. So Spenser has the noun in *The Faerie Queene*, iii. 9, 20: "Her golden locks, that were in *trammels* gay upbounden."—*Surcease* is, properly, a legal term, meaning the arrest or stay of a suit. So in Bacon's essay *Of Church Controversies*: "It is more than time that there were an end and *surcease* made of this immodest and deformed manner of writing," &c.—Here, as often, *success* probably has the sense of *sequel, succession*, or *succeeding events*. So that to *catch success* is to arrest and stop off all further outcome, or all entail of danger.

[105] To *jump* is to *risk*, to *hazard*. Repeatedly so.

[106] *That*, in old English, often has the force of *since*, or *inasmuch as*.

[107] *Faculties* in an official sense; honours, dignities, prerogatives, whatever pertains to his regal seat.

[108] "Sightless couriers of the air" means the same as what the Poet elsewhere calls "the viewless winds."—The metaphor of tears drowning the wind is taken from what we sometimes see in a thunder-shower; which is ushered in by a high wind; but, when the rain gets to falling hard, the wind subsides, as if strangled by the water.

[109] *Self* here stands for *aim* or *purpose*; as we often say, such a one *overshot himself* that is, overshot his *mark* or *aim*.

How now! what news?

LADY MACBETH. He has almost supp'd: why have you left the chamber?

MACBETH. Hath he ask'd for me?

LADY MACBETH. Know you not he has?

MACBETH. We will proceed no further in this business:
He hath honour'd me of late; and I have bought
Golden opinions from all sorts of people,
Which would[110] be worn now in their newest gloss,
Not cast aside so soon.

LADY MACBETH. Was the hope drunk
Wherein you dress'd yourself?[111] hath it slept since?
And wakes it now, to look so green and pale
At what it did so freely? From this time
Such I account thy love. Art thou afeard
To be the same in thine own act and valor
As thou art in desire? Wouldst thou have that
Which thou esteem'st the ornament of life,
And live a coward in thine own esteem;
Letting *I dare not* wait upon *I would*,
Like the poor cat i' the adage?[112]

MACBETH. Pr'ythee, peace!
I dare do all that may become a man;
Who dares do more is none.

LADY MACBETH. What beast[113] was't, then,
That made you break this enterprise to me?
When you durst do it, then you were a man;
And, to be more than what you were, you would
Be so much more the man. Nor time nor place
Did then adhere,[114] and yet you would make both:

---

[110] *Would* for *should*. The two were often used indiscriminately.

[111] Every student of Shakespeare knows that he often uses to address for to *make ready* or to *prepare*. And he repeatedly has the shortened form *dress* in the same sense. From oversight of this, some strange comments have been made upon the present passage, as if it meant that Macbeth had *put on* hope as a *dress*. The meaning I take to be something thus "Was it a drunken man's hope, *in the strength of which* you *made* yourself *ready* for the killing of Duncan? and does that hope now wake from its drunken sleep, to shudder and turn pale at the preparation which it made so freely?" In accordance with this explanation, the Lady's next speech shows that at some former time Macbeth had been, or had fancied himself, *ready* to *make* an opportunity for the murder.

[112] The adage of the cat is among Heywood's *Proverbs*, 1566: "The cat would eate fishe, and would not wet her feete."

[113] The word *beast* is exceedingly well chosen here: it conveys a stinging allusion to what Macbeth has just said: "If you dare do all that may become a *man*, then what *beast* was it that put this enterprise into your head?"

[114] *Adhere* in the sense of *cohere*; that is, *consist* with the purpose.—This passage

They have made themselves, and that their fitness now
Does unmake you. I have given suck, and know
How tender 'tis to love the babe that milks me:
I would, while it was smiling in my face,
Have pluck'd my nipple from his boneless gums
And dash'd the brains out, had I so sworn as you
Have done to this.[115]
MACBETH. If we should fail?
LADY MACBETH. We fail.[116]
But screw your courage to the sticking-place,[117]
And we'll not fail. When Duncan is asleep,—
Whereto the rather shall his day's hard journey
Soundly invite him, his two chamberlains
Will I with wine and wassail so convince,[118]
That memory, the warder of the brain,
Shall be a fume, and the receipt of reason
A limbeck only:[119] when in swinish sleep

---

infers that the murdering of Duncan had been a theme of conversation between Macbeth and his wife long before the weird salutation. He was then for making a time and place for the deed; yet, now that they have made themselves to his hand, he is unmanned by them.

[115] Lady Macbeth begins with acting a part which is really foreign to her; but which, notwithstanding, such is her energy of will, she braves out to issues so overwhelming, that her husband and many others believe it to be her own. It is said that Mrs. Siddons used to utter the closing words of this speech in a scream, as though scared from her propriety by the audacity of her own tongue. And I can well conceive how a spasmodic action of fear might lend to such a woman as Lady Macbeth an appearance of superhuman or inhuman boldness. At all events, it seems clear enough that in this case her fierce vehemence of purpose rasps her woman's feelings to the quick; and the pang thence resulting might well utter itself in a scream.

[116] The sense of this much-disputed passage I take to be simply this: "If we should fail, why, then, to be sure, we fail, and it is all over with us." So long as there is any hope or prospect of success, Lady Macbeth is for going ahead; and she has a mind to risk all and lose all, rather than let slip any chance of being queen. And why should she not be as ready to jump the present life in such a cause as her husband is to "jump the life to come"?

[117] A metaphor from *screwing up* the cords of stringed instruments to the proper tension, when the peg remains fast in its *sticking-place*.

[118] To *convince* is to *overcome* or *subdue.—Wassail* is an old word for *quaffing, carousing*, or drinking to one's health.

[119] The language and imagery of this strange passage are borrowed from the distillery, as it was in Shakespeare's time. *Limbeck* is alembic, the cap of a still, into which the fumes rise before passing into the condenser. *Receipt* is *receptacle*, or *receiver*. The old anatomists divided the brain into three ventricles, in the hindmost of which, the cerebellum, the memory was posted like a keeper or sentinel to warn the reason against attack. When by intoxication the memory is converted to a fume, the sphere of reason will be so filled therewith as to be like the receiver of a still; and in this state of the man all sense or intelligence of what has happened will be suffocated. Such appears to be the meaning of the passage; which is far from being a felicitous one. The Poet elsewhere uses *fume* thus; as in *Antony and Cleopatra*, ii. 1: "Tie up the libertine in a field of feasts, keep his brain *fuming*."

Their drenched natures lie as in a death,
What cannot you and I perform upon
The unguarded Duncan? what not put upon
His spongy[120] officers; who shall bear the guilt
Of our great quell?[121]

MACBETH. Bring forth men-children only;
For thy undaunted mettle should compose
Nothing but males. Will it not be receiv'd,
When we have mark'd with blood those sleepy two
Of his own chamber, and us'd their very daggers,
That they have done't?

LADY MACBETH. Who dares receive it other,[122]
As we shall make our griefs and clamor roar
Upon his death?

MACBETH. I am settled, and bend up
Each corporal agent to this terrible feat.
Away, and mock the time with fairest show:
False face must hide what the false heart doth know. [*Exeunt.*]

ACT II.

SCENE I.

Inverness. Court of MACBETH'*s Castle.*

[*Enter* BANQUO, *preceded by* FLEANCE *with a torch.*]

BANQUO. How goes the night, boy?
FLEANCE. The moon is down; I have not heard the clock.
BANQUO. And she goes down at twelve.
FLEANCE. I take't, 'tis later, sir.
BANQUO. Hold, take my sword.—There's husbandry[123] in Heaven;
Their candles are all out. Take thee that too.—
A heavy summons lies like lead upon me,
And yet I would not sleep:—merciful powers,
Restrain in me the cursed thoughts that nature
Gives way to in repose![124]

---

[120] *Spongy* because they soak up so much liquor.

[121] *Quell* is *murder*; from the Saxon *quellan*, to *kill*.

[122] That is, "Who will dare to *understand it otherwise?*"—As is here equivalent to *since* or *seeing that*.

[123] The heavens are *economizing* their light. *Frugality* or *economy* is one of the old senses of *husbandry*. *Heaven* is here a collective noun.

[124] It appears afterwards that Banquo has been dreaming of the Weird Sisters. He understands full well how their greeting may act as an incentive to crime, and shrinks with pious horror from the poison of such evil suggestions, and seeks refuge in prayer

[*Enter* MACBETH, *and a* SERVANT *with a torch.*]

      Give me my sword.—
Who's there?
MACBETH. A friend.
BANQUO. What, sir, not yet at rest? The king's a-bed:
    He hath been in unusual pleasure and
    Sent forth great largess to your officers:[125]
    This diamond he greets your wife withal,
    By the name of most kind hostess; and shut up[126]
    In measureless content.
MACBETH. Being unprepar'd,
    Our will became the servant to defect;[127]
    Which else should free have wrought.
BANQUO. All's well.
    I dreamt last night of the three weird sisters:
    To you they have show'd some truth.
MACBETH. I think not of them:
    Yet, when we can entreat an hour to serve,
    We would spend it in some words upon that business,
    If you would grant the time.
BANQUO. At your kind'st leisure.
MACBETH. If you shall cleave to my consent,[128] when 'tis,
    It shall make honour for you.
BANQUO. So I lose none
    In seeking to augment it, but still keep
    My bosom franchis'd, and allegiance clear,
    I shall be counsell'd.
MACBETH. Good repose the while!
BANQUO. Thanks, sir: the like to you!

[*Exeunt* BANQUO *and* FLEANCE.]

---

from the invasion of guilty thoughts even in his sleep. Herein his character stands in marked contrast with that of Macbeth, whose mind is inviting wicked thoughts, and catching eagerly at temptation, and revolving how he may work the guilty suggestions through into act.

[125] *Officers* are those having in charge the various branches of household work, such as cook, butler, &c.; as the several rooms used for those branches were called *offices*.

[126] *Shut up* probably means *composed himself to rest*. The phrase may be a little quaint; but I think it well expresses the act of closing one's mind to the cares and interests of the world.

[127] A man may be said to be the servant of that which he cannot help: and Macbeth means that his will would have made ampler preparation, but that it was fettered by want of time.

[128] Meaning, apparently, "If you will stick to my side, to what has my *consent*; if you will tie yourself to my fortunes and counsel."

MACBETH. Go bid thy mistress, when my drink is ready,
    She strike upon the bell. Get thee to bed.—[*Exit* SERVANT.]
    Is this a dagger which I see before me,
    The handle toward my hand? Come, let me clutch thee:—
    I have thee not, and yet I see thee still.
    Art thou not, fatal vision, sensible
    To feeling as to sight? or art thou but
    A dagger of the mind, a false creation,
    Proceeding from the heat-oppressed brain?
    I see thee yet, in form as palpable
    As this which now I draw. [*He draws his dagger.*]
    Thou marshall'st me the way that I was going;
    And such an instrument I was to use.
    Mine eyes are made the fools o' the other senses,
    Or else worth all the rest:[129] I see thee still;
    And on thy blade and dudgeon gouts of blood,
    Which was not so before.—There's no such thing:
    It is the bloody business which informs
    Thus to mine eyes.—Now o'er the one half-world
    Nature seems dead, and wicked dreams abuse
    The curtain'd sleep; now witchcraft celebrates
    Pale Hecate's offerings;[130] and wither'd murder,
    Alarum'd by his sentinel, the wolf,
    Whose howl's his watch,[131] thus with his stealthy pace,
    With Tarquin's ravishing strides,[132] towards his design
    Moves like a ghost.—Thou sure and firm-set earth,
    Hear not my steps, which way they walk, for fear
    Thy very stones prate of my whereabout,[133]
    And take the present horror from the time,
    Which now suits with it.[134] Whiles I threat, he lives;

---

[129] Senses is here used with a double reference, to the bodily organs of sense and the inward faculties of the mind. Either his eyes are deceived by his imaginative forces in being made to see that which is not, or else his other senses are at fault in not being able to find the reality which his eyes behold.—*Dudgeon*, next line, is the handle or haft of the dagger: *gouts* is drops; from the French *gouttes*.

[130] That is, makes offerings or sacrifices to Hecate, who was the Queen of Hades, the patroness of all infernal arts, and of course the mistress of all who practised them; here called *pale*, because, under the name of Diana, she was identified with the Moon.

[131] *Watch* is here used, apparently, for *signal*. The figure is of the wolf acting as the Sentinel of Murder, and his howl being the signal to give warning of approaching danger.

[132] *Strides* did not always carry the idea of violence or noise, but was used in a sense coherent enough with *stealthy pace*. So in *The Faerie Queene*, iv. 8, 37: "They passing forth kept on their readie way, with *easie* step so soft as foot could *stryde*."

[133] That is, "tell tales of where I have been," or "of my having been here." It seems to him as if the very stones might become apprehensive, divulge his dreadful secret, and witness against him.

Words to the heat of deeds too cold breath gives.

[*A bell rings.*]

I go, and it is done; the bell invites me.
Hear it not, Duncan, for it is a knell
That summons thee to heaven or to hell. [*Exit.*]

[*Enter* LADY MACBETH.]

LADY MACBETH. That which hath made them drunk hath made me
    bold:
What hath quench'd them hath given me fire.[135] Hark! Peace!
It was the owl that shriek'd, the fatal bellman,
Which gives the stern'st good-night.[136] He is about it:
The doors are open; and the surfeited grooms
Do mock their charge with snores: I have drugg'd their possets,
That death and nature do contend about them,
Whether they live or die.
MACBETH. [*Within.*] Who's there?—what, ho!
LADY MACBETH. Alack! I am afraid they have awak'd,
And 'tis not done: the attempt, and not the deed,
Confounds us.[137] Hark! I laid their daggers ready;
He could not miss 'em. Had he not resembled
My father as he slept, I had done't.[138]—My husband!

[*Enter* MACBETH.]

MACBETH. I have done the deed.—Didst thou not hear a noise?

---

[134] Macbeth would have nothing break through the universal silence that added such horror to the night, as well suited with the bloody deed he was about to perform. Burke, in his *Essay on the Sublime and Beautiful*, observes, that "all general privations are great because they are terrible."

[135] Lady Macbeth has fired her courage by drinking some wine; but, while she is kindled by drink, the grooms are stupefied, "their possets" having been drugged.

[136] The supposed ominousness of the owl's note is often alluded to by Shakespeare. The office of *bellman*, which the owl is here made to perform, is well explained in Webster's *Duchess of Malfi*: "I am the common bellman, that usually is sent to condemn'd persons the night before they suffer." Lady Macbeth of course regards Duncan as the condemned person to whom the "fatal bellman" gives "the stern'st good-night."

[137] "The attempt without the deed *destroys* or *ruins* us." The Poet often uses *confound* with this meaning.

[138] This little touch of nature is one of Shakespeare's most pregnant hints of character, and is enough of itself, I think, to upset the more common notion of Lady Macbeth. It tells us that, notwithstanding her appalling invocation to the "murdering ministers," her milk continues to be milk. And what a suggestive contrast it makes to the terrible audacity of thought and speech she has just displayed!

LADY MACBETH. I heard the owl scream and the crickets cry.
   Did not you speak?
MACBETH. When?
LADY MACBETH. Now.
MACBETH. As I descended?
LADY MACBETH. Ay.
MACBETH. Hark!—
   Who lies i' the second chamber?
LADY MACBETH. Donalbain.
MACBETH. [*Looking on his hands.*] This is a sorry sight.
LADY MACBETH. A foolish thought, to say a sorry sight.
MACBETH. There's one did laugh in's sleep, and one cried, "Murder!"
   That they did wake each other: I stood and heard them:
   But they did say their prayers, and address'd[139] them
   Again to sleep.
LADY MACBETH. There are two lodg'd together.
MACBETH. One cried, *God bless us!* and, *Amen*, the other;
   As they had seen me with these hangman's hands,[140]
   Listening their fear, I could not say *Amen*,
   When they did say, *God bless us.*
LADY MACBETH. Consider it not so deeply.
MACBETH. But wherefore could not I pronounce *Amen*?
   I had most need of blessing, and *Amen*
   Stuck in my throat.
LADY MACBETH. These deeds must not be thought
   After these ways; so, it will make us mad.
MACBETH. I heard a voice cry, *Sleep no more!*
   Macbeth does murder sleep;—the innocent sleep;
   Sleep that knits up the ravell'd sleave[141] of care,
   The death of each day's life, sore labour's bath,
   Balm of hurt minds, great nature's second course,
   Chief nourisher in life's feast.
LADY MACBETH. What do you mean?
MACBETH. Still it cried, *Sleep no more!* to all the house:
   Glamis hath murder'd sleep, and therefore Cawdor
   Shall sleep no more,—Macbeth shall sleep no more!
LADY MACBETH. Who was it that thus cried? Why, worthy thane,

---

[139] *Address'd* for *composed* or *prepared.* See page 42, note 111.

[140] "As *if* they had seen me with these *butcher's* hands." *As* for *as if* is very frequent.—*Hangman* was used for *executioner* in general, whether the work was done with rope or steel: hence, when beheading was common, the word contracted the sense of *butcher.*

[141] *Sleave* is an old name for soft floss silk, such as is used for weaving. So in Drayton's *Muses' Elysium*: "Grass as soft as *sleave* or sarcenet ever was." So that to "knit up the ravell'd sleave of care," is to compose and put in trim for use the soft silk that care has ravelled out or discomposed.

You do unbend your noble strength to think
So brainsickly of things.[142] Go get some water,
And wash this filthy witness from your hand.—
Why did you bring these daggers from the place?
They must lie there: go carry them; and smear
The sleepy grooms with blood.
MACBETH. I'll go no more:
I am afraid to think what I have done;
Look on't again I dare not.
LADY MACBETH. Infirm of purpose!
Give me the daggers: the sleeping and the dead
Are but as pictures: 'tis the eye of childhood
That fears a painted devil.[143] If he do bleed,
I'll gild the faces of the grooms withal,
For it must seem their guilt.[144] [*Exit. Knocking within.*]
MACBETH. Whence is that knocking?
How is't with me, when every noise appalls me?
What hands are here? Ha, they pluck out mine eyes!
Will all great Neptune's ocean wash this blood
Clean from my hand? No; this my hand will rather
The multitudinous seas incarnadine,
Making the green—one red.[145]

[*Re-enter* LADY MACBETH.]

LADY MACBETH. My hands are of your color, but I shame
To wear a heart so white. [*Knocking within.*] I hear knocking
At the south entry:—retire we to our chamber.
A little water clears us of this deed:
How easy is it then! Your constancy
Hath left you unattended.[146] [*Knocking within.*] Hark! more
knocking:
Get on your nightgown, lest occasion call us
And show us to be watchers:—be not lost

---

[142] *Brainsickly* is *insanely, crazily. Hamlet* has *brainish* in the same sense.—*To think* is equivalent to *in thinking*; an instance of the infinitive used gerundively, or like the Latin *gerund.*

[143] With her firm self-control, this bold woman, when awake, was to be moved by nothing but *facts*: when her powers of self-control were unknit by sleep, then was the time for her to see things that were not, save in her own conscience.

[144] Here we have a seeming quibble between *gild* and *guilt*. But I suspect the Poet did not mean it so. This use of to *gild* was very common, and so might slip in unconsciously.

[145] Making the green *water all* red. So in Milton's *Comus*: "And makes *one* blot of all the air."—To *incarnadine* is to *colour red.*

[146] That is, "Your firmness hath *forsaken* you, *doth not attend* you."

So poorly in your thoughts.
MACBETH. To know my deed, 'twere best not know myself.[147]—

[*Knocking within.*]

Wake Duncan with thy knocking! I would thou couldst! [*Exeunt.*]

[*Enter a* PORTER. *Knocking within.*]

PORTER. Here's a knocking indeed! If a man were porter of hell-gate,
he should have old[148] turning the key.—[*Knocking.*] Knock, knock,
knock. Who's there, i' the name of Beelzebub? *Here's a farmer
that hanged himself on the expectation of plenty.* Come in time;
have napkins[149] enow about you; here you'll sweat for't.—
[*Knocking.*] Knock, knock! Who's there, in the other devil's name?
*Faith, here's an equivocator, that could swear in both the scales
against either scale, who committed treason enough for God's
sake, yet could not equivocate to Heaven.*[150] O, come in,
equivocator. [*Knocking.*] Knock, knock, knock! Who's there?
*Faith, here's an English tailor come hither, for stealing out of a
French hose.*[151] Come in, tailor; here you may roast your goose.[152]
[*Knocking.*] Knock, knock: never at quiet! What are you?—But
this place is too cold for hell. I'll devil-porter it no further: I had
thought to have let in some of all professions, that go the primrose

---

[147] This is said in answer to Lady Macbeth's "Be not lost so poorly in your
thoughts"; and the meaning is, "While thinking of what I have done, it were best I should
be lost to myself, or should not know myself as the doer of it." Macbeth is now burnt
with the conscience of his deed, and would fain lose the memory of it. *To know* is another
gerundial infinitive, and so has the force of *in* or *while knowing*. See note 142.

[148] *Old* was a common intensive or augmentative, used much as *huge* is now.—The
Porter now proceeds to hold a dialogue with several imaginary persons at the door, who
are supposed to be knocking for admission to a warmer place.—Coleridge and several
others think this part of the scene could not have been written by Shakespeare. My
thinking is decidedly different. I am sure it is like him. Its broad drollery serves as a
proper foil to the antecedent horrors, and its very discordance with the surrounding matter
imparts an air of verisimilitude to the whole.

[149] In the old dictionaries *sudarium* is explained "*napkin* or *handkerchief*, wherewith
we wipe away the sweat."—"Come in time" probably means "you are welcome."

[150] "Could not equivocate *himself into* Heaven," or could not win Heaven by
equivocating, is the meaning.—To "swear in both the scales against either scale" is to
commit direct and manifest perjury.

[151] *Hose* was used for what we call *trousers*. Warburton says, "The joke consists in
this, that, a French hose being very short and strait, a tailor must be master of his trade
who could steal any thing from thence." Others say, perhaps more truly, that the allusion
is to a French fashion, which made the hose very large and wide, and so with more cloth
to be stolen.

[152] A tailor's *goose* is the heavy "flat-iron" with which he smoothes and presses his
work; so called because the handle bore some resemblance to the neck of a goose.

way to the everlasting bonfire.[153] [*Knocking.*] Anon, anon! I pray
you, remember the porter. [*Opens the gate.*]

[*Enter* MACDUFF *and* LENNOX.]

MACDUFF. Was it so late, friend, ere you went to bed,
That you do lie so late?
PORTER. Faith, sir, we were carousing till the second cock: and drink,
sir, is a great provoker of three things.
MACDUFF. What three things does drink especially provoke?
PORTER. Marry, sir, nose-painting, sleep, and urine. Lechery, sir, it
provokes and unprovokes; it provokes the desire, but it takes away
the performance: therefore much drink may be said to be an
equivocator with lechery: it makes him, and it mars him; it sets
him on, and it takes him off; it persuades him, and disheartens him;
makes him stand to, and not stand to: in conclusion, equivocates
him in a sleep, and giving him the lie, leaves him.
MACDUFF. I believe drink gave thee the lie last night.
PORTER. That it did, sir, i' the very throat o' me; but I requited him
for his lie; and, I think, being too strong for him, though he took up
my legs sometime, yet I made a shift to cast him.
MACDUFF. Is thy master stirring?—
Our knocking has awak'd him; here he comes.

[*Re-enter* MACBETH.]

LENNOX. Good morrow, noble sir!
MACBETH. Good morrow, both!
MACDUFF. Is the king stirring, worthy thane?
MACBETH. Not yet.
MACDUFF. He did command me to call timely on him:
I have almost slipp'd the hour.
MACBETH. I'll bring you to him.
MACDUFF. I know this is a joyful trouble to you;
But yet 'tis one.
MACBETH. The labour we delight in physics pain.[154]
This is the door.
MACDUFF. I'll make so bold to call.
For 'tis my limited[155] service. [*Exit.*]

---

[153] A bonfire at that date is invariably given in Latin Dictionaries as equivalent to
pyra or *rogus*; it was the fire for consuming the human body after death: and the hell-fire
differed from the earth-fire only in being everlasting. This use of a word so remarkably
descriptive in a double meaning is intensely Shakespearian.—FLEAY.

[154] To *heal*, to *cure*, to *relieve*, is an old meaning of to *physic*.

[155] The Poet repeatedly uses to *limit* in the exact sense of to *appoint*.

LENNOX. Goes the king hence to-day?

MACBETH. He does;—he did appoint so.[156]

LENNOX. The night has been unruly: where we lay,
    Our chimneys were blown down: and, as they say,
    Lamentings heard i' the air, strange screams of death;
    And prophesying, with accents terrible,
    Of dire combustion and confus'd events,
    New hatch'd to the woeful time: the obscure bird
    Clamour'd the live-long night:[157] some say the Earth
    Was feverous, and did shake.

MACBETH. 'Twas a rough night.

LENNOX. My young remembrance cannot parallel
    A fellow to it.[158]

[*Re-enter* MACDUFF.]

MACDUFF. O horror, horror, horror! Tongue nor heart
    Cannot conceive nor name thee!

MACBETH, LENNOX. What's the matter?

MACDUFF. Confusion[159] now hath made his masterpiece!
    Most sacrilegious murder hath broke ope
    The Lord's anointed temple,[160] and stole thence
    The life o' the building.

MACBETH. What is't you say? the life?

LENNOX. Mean you his majesty?

MACDUFF. Approach the chamber, and destroy your sight
    With a new Gorgon:—do not bid me speak;
    See, and then speak yourselves.—

[*Exeunt* MACBETH *and* LENNOX.]

    Awake, awake!—
    Ring the alarum bell:—murder and treason!

---

[156] Here we have a significant note of character. Macbeth catches himself in the utterance of a falsehood, which, I take it, is something at odds with his nature and habitual feelings; and he starts back into a mending of his speech, as from a spontaneous impulse to be true to himself. Much the same thing occurs before, when, upon his saying to his wife "Duncan comes here to-night," she asks, "And when goes hence?" and he replies, "To-morrow,—as he purposes."

[157] "The obscene bird" is the owl, which was regarded as a bird of ill omen, and is here represented as a prophet of the direful events in question. Obscene is used in its proper Latin sense, *ill-boding* or *portentous.*

[158] Here, as often, *fellow* is *equal.* To *parallel* is to *put alongside.*

[159] *Confusion* for *destruction*, as *confound* for *destroy*, before.

[160] In 1 Samuel, xxiv. 10, David speaks of King Saul as "the Lord's anointed"; and St. Paul calls Christians "the temple of the living God."

Banquo and Donalbain! Malcolm! awake!
Shake off this downy sleep, death's counterfeit,
And look on death itself! up, up, and see
The great doom's image![161] Malcolm! Banquo!
As from your graves rise up, and walk like sprites
To countenance this horror.[162] [*Alarum-bell rings.*]

[*Re-enter* LADY MACBETH.]

LADY MACBETH. What's the business,
    That such a hideous trumpet calls to parley
    The sleepers of the house? speak, speak!
MACDUFF. O gentle lady,
    'Tis not for you to hear what I can speak:
    The repetition, in a woman's ear,
    Would murder as it fell.—

[*Re-enter* BANQUO.]

        O Banquo, Banquo!
    Our royal master's murder'd!
LADY MACBETH. Woe, alas!
    What, in our house?[163]
BANQUO. Too cruel any where.—
    Dear Duff, I pr'ythee, contradict thyself,
    And say it is not so.

[*Re-enter* MACBETH *and* LENNOX.]

MACBETH. Had I but died an hour before this chance,
    I had liv'd a blessed time; for, from this instant
    There's nothing serious in mortality:[164]
    All is but toys: renown and grace is dead;
    The wine of life is drawn, and the mere lees
    Is left this vault to brag of.[165]

---

[161] "The great doom" means the judgment-clay, of which this occasion is regarded as a representation.

[162] "To countenance this horror" is to put on a likeness of it; to augment or intensify it; an effect which the further horror of men rising up as from the dead, and walking like ghosts, would naturally produce.

[163] Her ladyship's first thought appears to be, that she and her husband may be suspected of the murder.

[164] *Mortality* is here put for *humanity*, or the *state of human life*.

[165] Observe the fine links of association in *wine* and *vault*; the latter having a double reference, to the wine-vault and to the firmament over-arching the world of human life.

[*Enter* MALCOLM *and* DONALBAIN.]

DONALBAIN. What is amiss?
MACBETH. You are, and do not know't:
    The spring, the head, the fountain of your blood
    Is stopp'd; the very source of it is stopp'd.
MACDUFF. Your royal father's murder'd.
MALCOLM. O, by whom?
LENNOX. Those of his chamber, as it seem'd, had done't:
    Their hands and faces were all badg'd with blood;
    So were their daggers, which, unwip'd, we found
    Upon their pillows:
    They star'd, and were distracted; no man's life
    Was to be trusted with them.
MACBETH. O, yet I do repent me of my fury,
    That I did kill them.
MACDUFF. Wherefore did you so?
MACBETH. Who can be wise, amaz'd, temperate, and furious,
    Loyal and neutral, in a moment? No man:
    The expedition[166] of my violent love
    Outrun the pauser reason. Here lay Duncan,
    His silver skin lac'd with his golden blood;[167]
    And his gash'd stabs look'd like a breach in nature
    For ruin's wasteful entrance;[168] there, the murderers,
    Steep'd in the colours of their trade, their daggers
    Unmannerly breech'd with gore:[169] who could refrain,
    That had a heart to love, and in that heart
    Courage to make's love known?
LADY MACBETH. Help me hence, ho!
MACDUFF. Look to the lady.
MALCOLM. [*Aside to* DONALBAIN.] Why do we hold our tongues,
    That most may claim this argument for ours?
DONALBAIN. [*Aside to* MALCOLM.] What should be spoken
    Here, where our fate, Hid in an auger hole,[170]

---

[166] *Expedition* for *swiftness* or *haste*. Repeatedly so.

[167] To *gild* with blood is a very common phrase in old plays. Johnson says, "It is not improbable that Shakespeare put these forced and unnatural metaphors into the mouth of Macbeth, as a mark of artifice and dissimulation, to show the difference between the studied language of hypocrisy and the natural outcries of sudden passion. The whole speech, so considered, is a remarkable instance of judgment, as it consists entirely of antithesis and metaphor."

[168] The image is of a besieging army making a breach in the walls of a city, and thereby opening a way for general massacre and pillage.

[169] This probably means rudely covered, dressed, *trousered* with blood. A metaphor harsh and strained enough.

[170] "Where there is no hiding-place so small but that murder may be lurking therein,

May rush, and seize us? Let's away: our tears
Are not yet brew'd.
MALCOLM. [*Aside to* DONALBAIN.] Nor our strong sorrow
Upon the foot of motion.
BANQUO. Look to the lady:—

[LADY MACBETH *is carried out.*[171]]

And when we have our naked frailties hid,[172]
That suffer in exposure, let us meet,
And question this most bloody piece of work
To know it further. Fears and scruples shake us:
In the great hand of God I stand; and thence,
Against the undivulg'd pretense I fight
Of treasonous malice.[173]
MACDUFF. And so do I.
ALL. So all.
MACBETH. Let's briefly[174] put on manly readiness,
And meet i' the hall together.
ALL. Well contented.

[*Exeunt all but* MALCOLM *and* DONALBAIN.]

MALCOLM. What will you do? Let's not consort with them:
To show an unfelt sorrow is an office
Which the false man does easy. I'll to England.
DONALBAIN. To Ireland, I; our separated fortune
Shall keep us both the safer: where we are,
There's daggers in men's smiles: the near in blood,
The nearer bloody.[175]

---

ready to spring upon us at any moment." The Princes divine at once that their father has been murdered for the crown, and that the same motive means death to themselves as well.

[171] Some regard this swoon as feigned, others as real. The question is very material in the determining of Lady Macbeth's character. If feigned, why was it not done when the murder of Duncan was announced? The announcement of these additional murders takes her by surprise; she was not prepared for it; whereas in the other case she had, by her fearful energy of will, steeled her nerves up to it beforehand.

[172] Banquo and the others who slept in the castle have rushed forth undressed. This is what he refers to in "our naked frailties."

[173] The natural construction is, "and thence I fight against the undivulged pretense of treasonous malice." *Pretence* here means *intention* or *purpose*. A frequent usage. So the verb, a little further on: "What good could they *pretend?*"

[174] *Briefly*, here, is *quickly* or *speedily*. Often so.—"Manly readiness" probably means *man's attire*; the opposite of "naked frailties."

[175] Meaning that he suspects Macbeth, who is the next in blood, or kin.—The Poet sometimes uses the form of the positive with the sense of the comparative; which is

MALCOLM. This murderous shaft that's shot
    Hath not yet lighted;[176] and our safest way
    Is to avoid the aim. Therefore to horse;
    And let us not be dainty of leave-taking,[177]
    But shift away: there's warrant in that theft
    Which steals itself, when there's no mercy left. [*Exeunt.*]

SCENE II.

The Same. Without MACBETH's *Castle.*

[*Enter* ROSS *and an* OLD MAN.]

OLD MAN. Threescore and ten I can remember well:
    Within the volume of which time I have seen
    Hours dreadful and things strange; but this sore night
    Hath trifled former knowings.
ROSS. Ah, good father,
    Thou seest, the heavens, as troubled with man's act,
    Threaten his bloody stage: by the clock 'tis day,
    And yet dark night strangles the travelling lamp;
    Is't night's predominance, or the day's shame,
    That darkness does the face of earth entomb,
    When living light should kiss it?
OLD MAN. 'Tis unnatural,
    Even like the deed that's done. On Tuesday last,
    A falcon, towering in her pride of place,[178]
    Was by a mousing owl hawk'd at and kill'd.
ROSS. And Duncan's horse',[179]—a thing most strange and certain,—
    Beauteous and swift, the minions of their race,
    Turn'd wild in nature, broke their stalls, flung out,
    Contending 'gainst obedience, as they would make
    War with mankind.
OLD MAN. 'Tis said they eat each other.[180]
ROSS. They did so; to the amazement of mine eyes,
    That look'd upon't.

---

indicated here by the printing, *near'* for *nearer*.

[176] Suspecting this murder to be the work of Macbeth, Malcolm thinks it could have no purpose but what himself and his brother equally stand in the way of; that the shaft must pass through them to reach its mark.

[177] That is, *punctilious or particular about* leave-taking.

[178] A phrase in falconry for *soaring to the highest pitch.*

[179] *Horse'* for *horses.* Repeatedly so.

[180] Holinshed relates that, after King Duff's murder, "there was a *sparhawk* strangled by an *owl,*" and that "*horses* of *singular beauty* and *swiftness* did *eat their own flesh.*"

Here comes the good Macduff.

[*Enter* MACDUFF.]

How goes the world, sir, now?
MACDUFF. Why, see you not?
ROSS. Is't known who did this more than bloody deed?
MACDUFF. Those that Macbeth hath slain.
ROSS. Alas, the day!
What good could they pretend?
MACDUFF. They were suborn'd:
Malcolm and Donalbain, the king's two sons,
Are stol'n away and fled; which puts upon them
Suspicion of the deed.
ROSS. 'Gainst nature still:
Thriftless ambition, that wilt ravin up[181]
Thine own life's means!—Then 'tis most like,
The sovereignty will fall upon Macbeth.
MACDUFF. He is already nam'd; and gone to Scone
To be invested.
ROSS. Where is Duncan's body?
MACDUFF. Carried to Colme-kill,[182]
The sacred storehouse of his predecessors,
And guardian of their bones.
ROSS. Will you to Scone?
MACDUFF. No, cousin, I'll to Fife.
ROSS. Well, I will thither.[183]
MACDUFF. Well, may you see things well done there,—adieu!—
Lest our old robes sit easier than our new![184]
ROSS. Farewell, father.
OLD MAN. God's benison[185] go with you; and with those
That would make good of bad, and friends of foes! [*Exeunt.*]

---

[181] To *ravin up* is to consume or devour *ravenously.* The Poet elsewhere has *ravin down* in exactly the same sense.

[182] *Colme-kill* is the famous Iona, one of the Western Isles mentioned by Holinshed as the burial-place of many ancient kings of Scotland. *Colme-kill* means the *cell* or chapel of St. Columba.

[183] That is, "I will go to *Scone.*"

[184] This latter clause logically connects with "see things well done there"; *adieu!* being awkwardly thrust in for a rhyming couplet.

[185] *Benison* is *blessing,* and is used whenever the verse requires a trisyllable. The opposite sense was expressed by *malison.*

ACT III.

SCENE I.

Forres. A Room in the Palace.

[*Enter* BANQUO.]

BANQUO. Thou hast it now,—king, Cawdor, Glamis, all,
    As the weird women promis'd; and, I fear,
    Thou play'dst most foully for't; yet it was said
    It should not stand in thy posterity;
    But that myself should be the root and father
    Of many kings. If there come truth from them,—
    As upon thee, Macbeth, their speeches shine,[186]—
    Why, by the verities on thee made good,
    May they not be my oracles as well,
    And set me up in hope? But hush; no more.

[*Sennet sounded. Enter* MACBETH, *as the King*, LADY
    MACBETH, *as the Queen*; LENNOX, ROSS, LORDS,
    LADIES, *and* ATTENDANTS.]

MACBETH. Here's our chief guest.
LADY MACBETH. If he had been forgotten,
    It had been as a gap in our great feast,
    And all-thing unbecoming.[187]
MACBETH. To-night we hold a solemn supper,[188] sir,
    And I'll request your presence.
BANQUO. Let your highness
    Command upon me; to the which my duties
    Are with a most indissoluble tie
    For ever knit.
MACBETH. Ride you this afternoon?
BANQUO. Ay, my good lord.
MACBETH. We should have else desir'd your good advice,—
    Which still hath been both grave and prosperous,—
    In this day's council; but we'll take to-morrow.

---

[186] Their speeches *prosper*, or appear in the *lustre* of manifest truth; a conspicuous instance, to warrant belief in their predictions.
[187] That is, such an oversight would have disordered the whole feast, and rendered all things *unfitting* and *discordant*.
[188] This was the phrase of Shakespeare's time for a feast or banquet given to *solemnize* any event, as a birth, marriage, coronation.

Is't far you ride?

BANQUO. As far, my lord, as will fill up the time
  'Twixt this and supper: go not my horse the better,[189]
  I must become a borrower of the night,
  For a dark hour or twain.

MACBETH. Fail not our feast.

BANQUO. My lord, I will not.

MACBETH. We hear our bloody cousins are bestow'd
  In England and in Ireland; not confessing
  Their cruel parricide, filling their hearers
  With strange invention: but of that to-morrow;
  When therewithal we shall have cause of state
  Craving us jointly. Hie you to horse: adieu,
  Till you return at night. Goes Fleance with you?

BANQUO. Ay, my good lord: our time does call upon's.

MACBETH. I wish your horses swift and sure of foot;
  And so I do commend you to their backs.
  Farewell.—[*Exit* BANQUO.]
  Let every man be master of his time
  Till seven at night; to make society
  The sweeter welcome, we will keep ourself
  Till supper time alone: while then, God b' wi' you![190]—

[*Exeunt all but* MACBETH, *and an* ATTENDANT.]

  Sirrah, a word with you: attend those men
  Our pleasure?

ATTENDANT. They are, my lord, without the palace gate.

MACBETH. Bring them before us.—[*Exit Attendant.*]
    To be thus is nothing;
  But to be safely thus.[191] Our fears in[192] Banquo.
  Stick deep; and in his royalty of nature
  Reigns that which would[193] be fear'd: 'tis much he dares;
  And, to[194] that dauntless temper of his mind,

---

[189] Perhaps meaning, *If* my horse go not better *than usual*; but more likely, if my horse go not *too well*; that is, too well for the result in question. So the Poet often follows a well-known Latin idiom in his use of the comparative.

[190] "God be with you" is the original of our phrase *good bye*; and the text here aptly illustrates the process of the contraction.—*While* here means *until*; a sense in which it was often used.

[191] That is, "nothing, *without being* safely thus," or, "*unless we* be safely thus." The exceptive *but*, from *be out*, is used repeatedly so by the Poet.

[192] *In* for *on account of.*

[193] *Would*, again, for *should*. See page 42, note 110.—"Royalty of nature" is *royal* or *noble* nature. The Poet has many like forms of expression.

[194] *To*, again, for *in addition to.* See page 40, note 96.

He hath a wisdom that doth guide his valour
To act in safety. There is none but he
Whose being I do fear: and under him,
My genius is rebuk'd; as, it is said,
Mark Antony's was by Cæsar's.[195] He chid the sisters
When first they put the name of king upon me,
And bade them speak to him; then, prophet-like,
They hail'd him father to a line of kings:
Upon my head they plac'd a fruitless crown,
And put a barren sceptre in my gripe,
Thence to be wrench'd with an unlineal hand,
No son of mine succeeding. If't be so,
For Banquo's issue have I filed[196] my mind;
For them the gracious Duncan have I murder'd;
Put rancours in the vessel of my peace
Only for them; and mine eternal[197] jewel
Given to the common enemy of man,
To make them kings, the seed of Banquo kings!
Rather than so, come, fate, into the list,
And champion me to the utterance![198]—Who's there?—

[*Re-enter Attendant, with two Murderers.*]

Now go to the door, and stay there till we call.

[*Exit Attendant.*]

Was it not yesterday we spoke together?
FIRST MURDERER. It was, so please your highness.
MACBETH. Well then, now
Have you consider'd of my speeches? Know
That it was he, in the times past, which held you
So under fortune; which you thought had been

---

[195] Octavius Cæsar is the person referred to. In *Antony and Cleopatra*, ii. 3, *genius* is explained by the words *demon, angel*, and "thy *spirit* which keeps thee."

[196] *File* for *defile*. So in Wilkins's *Inforced Marriage*: "Oaths pass out of a man's mouth like smoke through a chimney, that *files* all the way it goes." *Foul* and *filth* are from the same original.

[197] "Eternal jewel" is immortal soul. So in *Othello*, iii. 3: "Or, by the worth of man's *eternal* soul."

[198] *Champion me* is *be my antagonist*, or fight it out with me in single combat; the only instance I have met with of *champion* so used.—To th' *utterance* is *to the uttermost*, or to the last extremity. So in Cotgrave: "*Combatre a oultrance*: To fight at sharp, to fight it out, or to the uttermost." So that the sense of the passage is, "Let Fate, that has decreed the throne to Banquo's issue, enter the lists in support of its own decrees, I will fight against it to the last extremity, whatever be the consequence."

Our innocent self: this I made good to you
In our last conference, pass'd in probation[199]
With you, how you were borne in hand;[200] how cross'd;
The instruments; who wrought with them;
And all things else that might to half a soul
And to a notion[201] craz'd say *Thus did Banquo.*
FIRST MURDERER. You made it known to us.
MACBETH. I did so; and went further, which is now
Our point of second meeting. Do you find
Your patience so predominant in your nature,
That you can let this go? Are you so gospell'd,
To pray[202] for this good man and for his issue,
Whose heavy hand hath bow'd you to the grave,
And beggar'd yours forever?
FIRST MURDERER. We are men, my liege.
MACBETH. Ay, in the catalogue ye go for men;
As hounds, and greyhounds, mongrels, spaniels, curs,
Shoughs, water-rugs, and demi-wolves are clept[203]
All by the name of dogs: the valu'd file[204]
Distinguishes the swift, the slow, the subtle,
The house-keeper, the hunter, every one
According to the gift which bounteous nature
Hath in him clos'd; whereby he does receive
Particular addition, from the bill
That writes them all alike: and so of men.
Now, if you have a station in the file,
Not i' the worst rank of manhood, say it;
And I will put that business in your bosoms,
Whose execution takes your enemy off;
Grapples you to the heart and love of us,
Who wear our health but sickly in his life,
Which in his death were perfect.
SECOND MURDERER. I am one, my liege,

---

[199] *Probation* here means *proof,* or rather *the act of proving.*

[200] To *bear in hand* is to *entourage* or *lead on* by false assurances and expectations. So used several times by the Poet.—In what follows, *cross'd* is *thwarted* or *baffled; instruments* is *agents;* and the general idea is, that Banquo has managed to hold up their hopes, while secretly preventing fruition; thus using them as tools, and cheating them out of their pay.

[201] *Notion* for *understanding* or *judgment.*

[202] Alluding to the Gospel precept, "Pray for them which despitefully use you." "So gospell'd *as* to pray," of course.

[203] *Shoughs* are *shaggy* dogs; now called *shocks.*—*Clept* is an old word for called. Shakespeare has it repeatedly so.

[204] "The *valued file*" is the *list* or *schedule* wherein their *value* and peculiar qualities are discriminated and set down.

Whom the vile blows and buffets of the world
Have so incens'd that I am reckless what
I do to spite the world.
FIRST MURDERER. And I another,
So weary with disasters, tugg'd with fortune,
That I would set my life on any chance,
To mend it or be rid on't.
MACBETH. Both of you
Know Banquo was your enemy.
BOTH MURDERERS. True, my lord.
MACBETH. So is he mine; and in such bloody distance,[205]
That every minute of his being thrusts
Against my near'st of life; and though I could
With barefac'd power sweep him from my sight,
And bid my will avouch it, yet I must not,
For[206] certain friends that are both his and mine,
Whose loves I may not drop, but wail his fall[207]
Who I myself struck down: and thence it is
That I to your assistance do make love;
Masking the business from the common eye
For sundry weighty reasons.
SECOND MURDERER. We shall, my lord,
Perform what you command us.
FIRST MURDERER. Though our lives—
MACBETH. Your spirits shine through you. Within this hour at most,
I will advise you where to plant yourselves;
Acquaint you with the perfect spy o' the time,[208]
The moment on't; for't must be done to-night
And something from the palace; always thought
That I require a clearness:[209] and with him,—
To leave no rubs[210] nor botches in the work,—
Fleance his son, that keeps him company,
Whose absence is no less material to me

---

[205] *Distance* here carries the sense of *degree*. It is a term of fencing for the space between the two antagonists. When men are in a hot mortal encounter with swords, they stand at just the right distance apart for the bloodiest strokes or thrusts. Hence the word came to be used for *enmity* in general.

[206] *For* is here *because of*, or *on account of*. Repeatedly so.

[207] The language is elliptical; the sense being "but *I must* wail."

[208] Will furnish you with an *exact and sure note* or *signal* of the time when to strike; which is probably done by or through the third murderer, who joins them just before the murder is done. The success of the undertaking depends on the assault being rightly timed. So that "the perfect *spy* of the time" is the *sure means of spying* or knowing the time.

[209] That is, "it being always borne in mind that I must stand clear of blame or suspicion."

[210] *Rubs* is *hindrances* or *impediments*.

Than is his father's, must embrace the fate
Of that dark hour. Resolve yourselves apart:
I'll come to you anon.
BOTH MURDERERS. We are resolv'd, my lord.
MACBETH. I'll call upon you straight: abide within.

[*Exeunt Murderers.*]

It is concluded:—Banquo, thy soul's flight,
If it find heaven, must find it out to-night. [*Exit.*]

SCENE II.

The same. Another Room in the Palace.

[*Enter* LADY MACBETH *and a Servant.*]

LADY MACBETH. Is Banquo gone from court?
SERVANT. Ay, madam, but returns again to-night.
LADY MACBETH. Say to the king, I would attend his leisure[211]
    For a few words.
SERVANT. Madam, I will. [*Exit.*]
LADY MACBETH. Naught's had, all's spent,
    Where our desire is got without content:
    'Tis safer to be that which we destroy,
    Than, by destruction, dwell in doubtful joy.

[*Enter* MACBETH.]

How now, my lord! why do you keep alone,
Of sorriest fancies your companions making;
Using those thoughts which should indeed have died
With them they think on? Things without[212] all remedy
Should be without regard: what's done is done.
MACBETH. We have scotch'd[213] the snake, not kill'd it;
    She'll close, and be herself; whilst our poor malice
    Remains in danger of her former tooth.
    But let the frame of things disjoint,
    Both the worlds suffer,
    Ere we will eat our meal in fear, and sleep
    In the affliction of these terrible dreams

---

[211] "Attend his leisure" is *wait* for him to be at leisure.
[212] Here, as often, *without* is *beyond.*
[213] *Scotch'd* is *scored* or *cut.* So in *Coriolanus,* iv. 5: "Before Corioli he *scotch'd*
and *notch'd* him like a carbonado."

That shake us nightly:[214] better be with the dead,
Whom we, to gain our peace, have sent to peace,
Than on the torture of the mind to lie
In restless ecstasy.[215] Duncan is in his grave;
After life's fitful fever he sleeps well;
Treason has done his worst: nor steel, nor poison,
Malice domestic, foreign levy, nothing,
Can touch him further.
LADY MACBETH. Come on;
Gently my lord, sleek o'er your rugged looks;
Be bright and jovial 'mong your guests to-night.
MACBETH. So shall I, love;
And so, I pray, be you: let your remembrance
Apply[216] to Banquo; present him eminence, both
With eye and tongue:[217] unsafe the while, that we
Must lave our honours in these flattering streams;[218]
And make our faces vizards to our hearts,
Disguising what they are.
LADY MACBETH. You must leave this.
MACBETH. O, full of scorpions is my mind, dear wife!
Thou know'st that Banquo, and his Fleance, live.[219]
LADY MACBETH. But in them nature's copy's not eterne.[220]
MACBETH. There's comfort yet; they are assailable;
Then be thou jocund: ere the bat hath flown
His cloister'd[221] flight, ere to black Hecate's summons,

---

[214] What "these terrible dreams" are, is shown in Lady Macbeth's sleepwalking agonies. It is of her state of mind, not of his own, that Macbeth is here thinking.

[215] *Ecstasy* is any violent perturbation of mind; *frenzy*, or *madness*.

[216] Here *apply* has the force of attach itself. So in *Antony* and *Cleopatra*, v. 2: "If you *apply yourself* to our intents,—which towards you are most gentle,—you shall find a benefit in this change."

[217] "Treat him with the highest consideration, or as the most eminent of our guests." Rather strange language, and not very happy withal; but such appears to be the meaning.—Is this a piece of irony? or is it meant as a blind, to keep his wife ignorant and innocent of the new crime on foot? I suspect he is trying to jest off the pangs of remorse.

[218] *Flattering streams is streams of flattery.* The meaning is, "The very fact of our being obliged thus to use the arts of hypocrisy and dissimulation proves that we are not safe in our seats, not secure in the tenure of our honours: we can retain them only by making our life, even in social intercourse, a studied, continuous lie."

[219] Macbeth mistranslates the recoilings and ominous whispers of conscience into prudential and selfish reasonings, and, after the deed is done, the terrors of remorse into fear from external dangers; like delirious men who run away from the phantoms of their own brains, or, raised by terror to rage, stab the real object that is within their reach.—
COLERIDGE.

[220] Ritson has justly observed that nature's *copy* alludes to *copyhold* tenure; in which the tenant holds an estate for *life*, having nothing but the *copy* of the rolls of his lord's court to show for it. A *life-hold* tenure may be well said to be not *eternal.*

[221] The bats wheeling round the dim cloisters of Queen's College, Cambridge, have frequently impressed on me the singular propriety of this original epithet.—STEEVENS.

The shard-borne beetle[222] with his drowsy hums,
Hath rung night's yawning peal, there shall be done
A deed of dreadful note.
LADY MACBETH. What's to be done?
MACBETH. Be innocent of the knowledge, dearest chuck,
Till thou applaud the deed.—Come, seeling[223] night,
Scarf up the tender eye of pitiful day;
And with thy bloody and invisible hand
Cancel and tear to pieces that great bond
Which keeps me paled![224]—Light thickens; and the crow
Makes wing to the rooky wood:[225]
Good things of day begin to droop and drowse;
Whiles night's black agents[226] to their preys do rouse.
Thou marvell'st at my words: but hold thee still;
Things bad begun make strong themselves by ill:
So, pr'ythee, go with me. [*Exeunt.*]

SCENE III.

The Same. A Park with a gate leading to the Palace.

[*Enter three* MURDERERS.]

FIRST MURDERER. But who did bid thee join with us?
THIRD MURDERER. Macbeth.
SECOND MURDERER. He needs not our mistrust;[227] since he delivers

---

[222] *Shard* or *sherd* is an old word for *scale*. So that "the shard-borne beetle" is the beetle borne along the air by its *shards* or *scaly* wings.—"Night's yawning-peal" is the nocturnal signal for going to sleep.

[223] *Seeling* is *blinding*; a term in Falconry. To *seel* the eyes of a hawk was to close them by sewing the eyelids together.

[224] "That great *bond*" is Banquo's life; the "copyhold tenure" of note 220.—*Paled* is shut in or confined with *palings*. As Macbeth afterwards puts it, Banquo's life has the effect of keeping him "cabin'd, cribb'd, confined, bound-in to saucy doubts and fears."

[225] To *thicken* seems to have been a common expression for *to grow dark*. So in Fletcher's Faithful Shepherdess: "Fold your flocks up, for the air 'gins to *thicken*."—*Crow* and *rook* were used of the same bird. So that the meaning is, the crows are hastening to their nightly resort, the wood where they gather for society and sleep.

[226] A covert allusion to the exploit which Macbeth's murderers are going about. He seems to want that his wife should suspect the new crime he has in hand, while he shrinks from telling her of it distinctly. And the purpose of his dark hints probably is, to prepare her, as far as may be, for a further strain upon her moral forces, which he sees to be already overstrained. For he fears that, if she has full knowledge beforehand of the intended murder, she may oppose it, and that, if she has no suspicion of it, the shock may be too much for her.

[227] The meaning is, "We need not mistrust him"; his perfect knowledge of what is to be done, and how, being a sufficient guaranty of his right to be with them.—Mr. A. P. Paton has lately made a strong argument to the point that the third murderer is Macbeth

Our offices and what we have to do
To the direction just.
FIRST MURDERER. Then stand with us.
The west yet glimmers with some streaks of day:
Now spurs the lated traveller apace,[228]
To gain the timely inn; and near approaches
The subject of our watch.
THIRD MURDERER. Hark! I hear horses.
BANQUO. [*Within.*] Give us a light there, ho!
SECOND MURDERER. Then 'tis he; the rest
That are within the note of expectation[229]
Already are i' the court.
FIRST MURDERER. His horses go about.
THIRD MURDERER. Almost a mile; but he does usually,
So all men do, from hence to the palace gate
Make it their walk.
SECOND MURDERER. A light, a light!
THIRD MURDERER. 'Tis he.
FIRST MURDERER. Stand to't.

[*Enter* BANQUO, *and* FLEANCE *with a torch.*]

BANQUO. It will be rain to-night.
FIRST MURDERER. Let it come down.

[*Assaults* BANQUO.]

BANQUO. O, treachery! Fly, good Fleance, fly, fly, fly!
Thou mayst revenge.—O slave! [*Dies.* FLEANCE *escapes.*]
THIRD MURDERER. Who did strike out the light?

---

himself in disguise. The thing sounds rather startling indeed, yet I am by no means sure but he is right. I can but condense a portion of his argument: That, although the banquet was to be at seven, Macbeth was not there till near midnight: That he has hardly more than entered the room before the murderer is at the door: That the third murderer repeats the precise directions given to the other two, and has perfect knowledge of the place, and the habits of visitors: That at the banquet Macbeth plays with the murderer at the door, as if exulting in the success of his disguise: That, when the Ghost rises, he asks the company, "Which of you have done this?" as if to take suspicion off himself, and says, in effect, to the Ghost, "In you black struggle you could never know me."—For the matter of this note, I am indebted, directly, to Mr. Furness's variorum edition of the play. Perhaps the strongest point against the writer's view is, that Macbeth seems surprised, and goes into a rapture, on being told that "Fleance is 'scaped"; but this may not be very much; he may there be feigning. On the other hand, Macbeth's actual sharing in the deed of murder would go far to account for his terrible hallucination at the banquet.

[228] *Lated* is the same as *belated.—Apace* is *rapidly.*—"To gain the *timely* inn," is to gain the inn *in time.*

[229] Whose names are in the list of those expected at the banquet.

FIRST MURDERER. Was't not the way?
THIRD MURDERER. There's but one down: the son is fled.
SECOND MURDERER. We have lost best half of our affair.
FIRST MURDERER. Well, let's away, and say how much is done.
    [*Exeunt.*]

SCENE IV.

The Same. A Room of State in the Palace.

[*A banquet prepared. Enter* MACBETH, LADY MACBETH, ROSS,
LENNOX, LORDS, *and* ATTENDANTS.]

MACBETH. You know your own degrees: sit down. At first
    And last the hearty welcome.
LORDS. Thanks to your majesty.
MACBETH. Ourself will mingle with society,
    And play the humble host. Our hostess keeps her state;[230]
    But in best time we will require her welcome.
LADY MACBETH. Pronounce it for me, sir, to all our friends;
    For my heart speaks they are welcome.

[FIRST MURDERER *appears at the door.*]

MACBETH. See, they encounter thee with their hearts' thanks.—
    Both sides are even: here I'll sit i' the midst:
    Be large in mirth; anon we'll drink a measure
    The table round. [*Goes to the door.*] There's blood upon thy face.
MURDERER. 'Tis Banquo's then.
MACBETH. 'Tis better thee without than he within.[231]
    Is he despatch'd?
MURDERER. My lord, his throat is cut; that I did for him.
MACBETH. Thou art the best o' the cut-throats; yet he's good
    That did the like for Fleance: if thou didst it,
    Thou art the nonpareil.
MURDERER. Most royal sir,
    Fleance is 'scap'd.
MACBETH. Then comes my fit again: I had else been perfect;
    Whole as the marble, founded as the rock;
    As broad and general as the casing[232] air:

---

[230] Her *chair* of state; which was a royal chair with a canopy over it.—*Require*, in the next line, is *request*. A frequent usage.

[231] "'Tis better on your outside than in his body."

[232] *Casing* is *enclosing, surrounding.* So *case*, substantive, was often used of any outer integument or cover, as the skin.—"Broad and general" is having full and free

But now I am cabin'd, cribb'd, confin'd, bound in
To saucy doubts and fears. But Banquo's safe?
MURDERER. Ay, my good lord: safe in a ditch he bides,
With twenty trenched gashes on his head;
The least a death to nature.
MACBETH. Thanks for that:
There the grown serpent lies; the worm[233] that's fled
Hath nature that in time will venom breed,
No teeth for the present.—Get thee gone; to-morrow
We'll hear, ourselves, again. [*Exit* MURDERER.]
LADY MACBETH. My royal lord,
You do not give the cheer: the feast is sold
That is not often vouch'd, while 'tis a-making,
'Tis given with welcome:[234] to feed were best at home;
From thence the sauce to meat is ceremony;[235]
Meeting were bare without it.
MACBETH. Sweet remembrancer!—
Now, good digestion wait on appetite,
And health on both!
LENNOX. May't please your highness sit.

[*The Ghost of* BANQUO[236] *enters, and sits in* MACBETH's
place.]

MACBETH. Here had we now our country's honour roof'd,
Were the grac'd person of our Banquo present;
Who may I rather challenge for unkindness
Than pity for mischance!
ROSS. His absence, sir,

---

scope; *unclogged.*

[233] *Worm* and *serpent* were used synonymously.

[234] The last clause depends on *vouch'd*; "that is not often declared to be given with
welcome."—"The feast is sold," that is, made or given for profit, not as a frank
expression of kindness and good-will.

[235] If merely to feed were all, that were best done at home: away from home, words
and acts of courtesy are what give relish to food.

[236] The actual reappearance of the murdered Banquo on the stage, in this scene, has
long appeared to me a stark anachronism. It can hardly fail to excite feelings just the
reverse of suitable to the occasion. It is indeed certain, from Forman's *Notes*, that such
reappearance was used in the Poet's time; but there were good reasons for it then which
do not now exist. In the right conception of the matter, the ghost is manifestly a thing
existing only in the diseased imagination of Macbeth; what we call a *subjective* ghost, a
Banquo of the mind; and having no more objective being than the air-drawn dagger of a
previous scene; the difference being that Macbeth is there so well in his senses as to be
aware of the unreality, while he is here quite out of his senses, and completely
hallucinated. All this is evident in that the apparition is seen by none of the other persons
present. In Shakespeare's time, the generality of people could not possibly take the
conception of a subjective ghost; but it is not so now.

Lays blame upon his promise. Please't your highness
To grace us with your royal company?
MACBETH. The table's full.
LENNOX. Here is a place reserv'd, sir.
MACBETH. Where?
LENNOX. Here, my good lord. What is't that moves your highness?
MACBETH. Which of you have done this?
LORDS. What, my good lord?
MACBETH. [*to the* GHOST.] Thou canst not say I did it: never shake
Thy gory locks at me.
ROSS. Gentlemen, rise; his highness is not well.
LADY MACBETH. Sit, worthy friends:—my lord is often thus,
And hath been from his youth: pray you, keep seat;
The fit is momentary; upon a thought
He will again be well: if much you note him,
You shall[237] offend him, and extend his passion:
Feed, and regard him not.—Are you a man?
MACBETH. Ay, and a bold one, that dare look on that
Which might appal the devil.
LADY MACBETH. [*Aside to* MACBETH.]O proper stuff!
This is the very painting of your fear:
This is the air-drawn dagger which, you said,
Led you to Duncan. O, these flaws, and starts,—
Impostors to true fear,[238] would well become
A woman's story at a winter's fire,
Authoriz'd by her grandam. Shame itself!
Why do you make such faces? When all's done,
You look but on a stool.
MACBETH. Pr'ythee, see there! behold! look! lo! how say you?—
Why, what care I? If thou canst nod, speak too.—
If charnel houses and our graves must send
Those that we bury back, our monuments
Shall be the maws of kites.[239] [GHOST *disappears.*]
LADY MACBETH. What, quite unmann'd in folly?
MACBETH. If I stand here, I saw him.

---

[237] In Shakespeare's time, the auxiliaries *shall* and *will*, like *could, should*, and *would*, were often used indiscriminately. The same usage has occurred several times before in this play.

[238] The meaning probably is, that these hysterical gusts and jerks of fear at unrealities are mere *counterfeits* of the true fear that springs from real dangers; such counterfeits as *impose upon*, or *act the impostor to*, those who give way to them. Or it may be that here, as often, *to* has the force of *compared to*.

[239] The same thought occurs in *The Faerie Queene*, ii. 8, 16: "But be entombed in the raven or the *kite*." Also in Fairfax's Tasso, xii. 79: "Let that self monster me in pieces rend, and deep entomb me in his hollow chest." And an ancient author calls vultures "living sepulchres."

LADY MACBETH. Fie, for shame!

MACBETH. Blood hath been shed ere now, i' the olden time,
    Ere humane statute purg'd the gentle weal,[240]
    Ay, and since too, murders have been perform'd
    Too terrible for the ear: the time has been,
    That, when the brains were out, the man would die,
    And there an end; but now they rise again,
    With twenty mortal murders on their crowns,
    And push us from our stools: this is more strange
    Than such a murder is.

LADY MACBETH. My worthy lord,
    Your noble friends do lack you.

MACBETH. I do forget.—
    Do not muse[241] at me, my most worthy friends;
    I have a strange infirmity, which is nothing
    To those that know me. Come, love and health to all;
    Then I'll sit down.—Give me some wine, fill full.—
    I drink to the general joy o' the whole table,
    And to our dear friend Banquo, whom we miss:
    Would he were here! to all, and him, we thirst,
    And all to all.[242]

LORDS. Our duties, and the pledge.

[*Re-enter the* GHOST.[243]]

MACBETH. Avaunt! and quit my sight! let the earth hide thee!
    Thy bones are marrowless, thy blood is cold;
    Thou hast no speculation[244] in those eyes
    Which thou dost glare with!

---

[240] The meaning is, ere humane statute made the commonwealth gentle by purging and cleansing it from the wrongs and pollutions of barbarism, Another prolepsis. See page 39, note 88.—The sense of *gentle*, here, is *civil*, *sociable*, amendable to order and law.

[241] Shakespeare uses to *muse* for to *wonder*, to be *amazed*.

[242] I am not clear as to the precise meaning of this: probably it is, "We crave to drink to the health of all, and of him, and to have every one present join in the pledge to all."

[243] Much question has been made, whether there be not two several ghosts in this scene; some maintaining that Duncan's enters here, and Banquo's before; others, that Banquo's enters here, and Duncan's before. The question is best disposed of by referring to Dr. Forman, who, as he speaks of Banquo's ghost, would doubtless have spoken of Duncan's, had there been any such: "The night, being at supper with his noblemen, whom he had bid to a feast, (to the which also Banquo should have come,) he began to speak of noble Banquo, and to wish that he were there. And as he thus did, *standing up to drink a carouse to him, the ghost of Banquo* came and sat down in his chair behind him. And he, turning about to sit down again, *saw the ghost of Banquo*, which fronted him, so that he fell in a great passion of fear and fury."

[244] *Speculation* in its proper Latin sense of *vision* or *seeing*.

LADY MACBETH. Think of this, good peers,
But as a thing of custom: 'tis no other,
Only it spoils the pleasure of the time.
MACBETH. What man dare, I dare:
Approach thou like the rugged Russian bear,
The arm'd[245] rhinoceros, or the Hyrcan tiger;
Take any shape but that, and my firm nerves
Shall never tremble: or be alive again,
And dare me to the desert with thy sword;
If trembling I inhabit then,[246] protest me
The baby of a girl.[247] Hence, horrible shadow!
Unreal mockery, hence! [GHOST *disappears*.]
     Why, so;—being gone,
I am a man again.—Pray you, sit still.
LADY MACBETH. You have displaced the mirth, broke the good
     meeting,
With most admired[248] disorder.
MACBETH. Can such things be,
And overcome us like a summer's cloud,
Without our special wonder?[249] You make me strange
Even to the disposition that I owe,[250]
When now I think you can behold such sights,
And keep the natural ruby of your cheeks,
When mine are blanch'd with fear.
ROSS. What sights, my lord?
LADY MACBETH. I pray you, speak not; he grows worse and worse;
Question enrages him: at once, good-night:—
Stand not upon the order of your going,[251]
But go at once.
LENNOX. Good-night; and better health

---

[245] *Arm'd* for *armoured*, referring to the thickness and hardness of the animal's hide.

[246] This passage is explained by Home Tooke: "Dare me to the desert with thy sword; if then I do not meet thee there; if trembling I stay in my castle, or any *habitation*; If I then hide my head, or *dwell* in any place through fear, protest me the baby of a girl." Milton uses *inhabit* in a similar sense, *Paradise Lost*, vii.. "Meanwhile *inhabit* lax, ye Powers of Heaven." The usage was not uncommon.

[247] "The baby of a girl," some say, is a girl's baby; that is, a doll. Others think it means the child of an immature mother. I suspect it means simply a *babyish* girl. We have many like phrases; as "a wonder of a man"; that is, a *wonderful* man. This explanation was proposed to me by Professor Howison of Boston.

[248] *Admired* for *admirable*, and in the Latin sense of *wonderful*.

[249] *Pass over* us without our wonder, as a casual Summer's cloud passes unregarded.

[250] "I have hitherto supposed myself a man of firm courage; but that you should now be perfectly unmoved when I am so shaken with terror, makes me doubtful of my own disposition. I seem a stranger to myself, and cannot tell what I am made of."

[251] Stay not to go out according to your rank or order of precedence.

Attend his majesty!
LADY MACBETH. A kind good-night to all!

[*Exeunt all but* MACBETH *and* LADY MACBETH.]

MACBETH. It will have blood; they say, blood will have blood:
  Stones have been known to move, and trees to speak;
  Augurs, and understood relations,[252] have
  By maggot-pies, and choughs, and rooks, brought forth
  The secret'st man of blood.—What is the night?
LADY MACBETH. Almost at odds with morning, which is which.
MACBETH. How say'st thou,[253] that Macduff denies his person
  At our great bidding?
LADY MACBETH. Did you send to him, sir?
MACBETH. I hear it by the way; but I will send:
  There's not a one of them but in his house
  I keep a servant fee'd.[254] I will to-morrow,
  (And betimes I will) to the weird sisters:
  More shall they speak; for now I am bent to know,
  By the worst means, the worst. For mine own good,
  All causes shall give way: I am in blood
  Step't in so far that, should I wade no more,
  Returning were as tedious as go o'er:
  Strange things I have in head, that will to hand;
  Which must be acted ere they may be scann'd.
LADY MACBETH. You lack the season[255] of all natures, sleep.
MACBETH. Come, we'll to sleep. My strange and self-abuse
  Is the initiate fear,[256] that wants hard use:—

---

[252] A passage very obscure to general readers, but probably intelligible enough to those experienced in the course of criminal trials; where two or three little facts or items of testimony may be of no significance taken singly or by themselves; yet, when they are put together and their relations *understood*, they may be enough to convict or acquit the accused. And even so trifling a matter as the note or talk of a parrot, interpreted in the light of such relations, may prove decisive of the case. *Magot-pie* or *magpie* and *chough* are old words for *parrot* or *parraquito.*

[253] "What do you say *of* this *fact* or *circumstance?*"—By "our great bidding" is meant, not any particular request or order to Macduff, but the *general invitation* implied in the very purpose of the banquet. Macbeth has heard of his refusal only "by the way," that is, *incidentally*, or through a "fee'd servant." Such is the substance of Elwin's explanation as given in Mr. Furness's *Variorum.*—See, below, page 75, note 265.

[254] Meaning that he has paid spies lurking and prowling about in the families of all the noblemen, and using the advantage of their place as servants to get information for him. The meanest and hatefullest practice of a jealous tyrant!

[255] Johnson explains this, "*You want sleep*, which *seasons* or gives the *relish* to all natures." So in *Cymbeline*, i. 6: "Blest be those, how mean soe'er, that have their honest wills; which *seasons* comfort."

[256] The *initiate fear* is the fear that attends the first stages of guilt.—The *and* in this speech is redundant. The Poet continually uses *abuse* for *delusion* or *deception.* So, here,

We are yet but young in deed. [*Exeunt.*]

SCENE V.

A Heath. Thunder.

[*Enter the three* WITCHES, *meeting* HECATE.]

FIRST WITCH. Why, how now, Hecate? you look angerly.
HECATE. Have I not reason, beldams as you are,
  Saucy and overbold? How did you dare
  To trade and traffic with Macbeth
  In riddles and affairs of death;
  And I, the mistress of your charms,
  The close[257] contriver of all harms,
  Was never call'd to bear my part,
  Or show the glory of our art?
  And, which is worse, all you have done
  Hath been but for a wayward son,
  Spiteful and wrathful; who, as others do,
  Loves for his own ends, not for you.
  But make amends now: get you gone,
  And at the pit of Acheron
  Meet me i' the morning: thither he
  Will come to know his destiny.
  Your vessels and your spells provide,
  Your charms, and everything beside.
  I am for the air; this night I'll spend
  Unto a dismal and a fatal end.
  Great business must be wrought ere noon:
  Upon the corner of the moon
  There hangs a vaporous drop profound;[258]
  I'll catch it ere it come to ground:
  And that, distill'd by magic sleights,[259]
  Shall raise such artificial sprites,
  As, by the strength of their illusion,
  Shall draw him on to his confusion:

---

self-abuse is *self-delusion*. Macbeth now knows that the Banquo he has just seen was but a Banquo of the mind.

[257] Here, as often, *close* is *secret* or *unseen*.

[258] *Profound* here signifies having deep or secret qualities. The *vaporous drop* seems to have been the same as the *virus lunare* of the ancients, being a foam which the Moon was supposed to shed on particular herbs, or other objects, when strongly solicited by enchantments.

[259] *Sleights* is *arts*, or *subtle practices*: as in the phrase, "sleight of hand."

He shall spurn fate, scorn death, and bear
His hopes 'bove wisdom, grace, and fear:
And you all know, security[260]
Is mortals' chiefest enemy.

[*Music and song within, "Come away, come away" &c.*[261]]

Hark! I am call'd; my little spirit, see,
Sits in a foggy cloud and stays for me. [*Exit.*]
FIRST WITCH. Come, let's make haste; she'll soon be back again.
[*Exeunt.*]

SCENE VI.

Forres. A Room in the Palace.

[*Enter* LENNOX *and another* LORD.]

LENNOX. My former speeches have but hit your thoughts,
 Which can interpret further: only, I say,
 Thing's have been strangely borne. The gracious Duncan
 Was pitied of Macbeth:—marry, he was dead:—
 And the right valiant Banquo walk'd too late;
 Whom, you may say, if't please you, Fleance kill'd,
 For Fleance fled. Men must not walk too late.
 Who cannot want the thought,[262] how monstrous
 It was for Malcolm and for Donalbain
 To kill their gracious father? damned fact!
 How it did grieve Macbeth! did he not straight,
 In pious rage, the two delinquents tear
 That were the slaves of drink and thralls of sleep?
 Was not that nobly done? Ay, and wisely too;
 For 'twould have anger'd any heart alive,
 To hear the men deny't. So that, I say,
 He has borne all things well: and I do think,
 That had he Duncan's sons under his key,—
 As, an't please heaven, he shall not,—they should find
 What 'twere to kill a father; so should Fleance.
 But, peace!—for from broad[263] words, and 'cause he fail'd

---

[260] *Security* in the Latin sense of *over-confidence* or *presumption*. Both the noun and the adjective are often used thus.

[261] For the rest of the song used here.

[262] An old form of speech, meaning "*be without* the thought," or *lack* it. We should say, "Who can *help thinking?*"

[263] *Broad*, here, is *plain, outright, free-spoken.*

His presence at the tyrant's feast, I hear,
Macduff lives in disgrace. Sir, can you tell
Where he bestows himself?
LORD. The son of Duncan,
From whom this tyrant holds the due of birth,
Lives in the English court and is receiv'd
Of the most pious Edward with such grace
That the malevolence of fortune nothing
Takes from his high respect: thither Macduff
Is gone to pray the holy king, upon his aid
To wake Northumberland, and warlike Siward:
That, by the help of these,—with Him above
To ratify the work,—we may again
Give to our tables meat, sleep to our nights;
Free from our feasts and banquets bloody knives;
Do faithful homage, and receive free honours,—
All which we pine for now: and this report
Hath so exasperate[264] the king that he
Prepares for some attempt of war.
LENNOX. Sent he to Macduff?
LORD. He did: and with an absolute *Sir, not I,*
The cloudy messenger turns me his back,
And hums, as who should say,[265] *You'll rue the time*
That clogs me with this answer.
LENNOX. And that well might
Advise him to a caution, to hold what distance
His wisdom can provide. Some holy angel
Fly to the court of England, and unfold
His message ere he come; that a swift blessing
May soon return to this our suffering country
Under a hand accursed![266]
LORD. I'll send my prayers with him. [*Exeunt.*]

---

[264] *Exasperate* for *exasperated*. The Poet has many such shortened preterites; as *consecrate, contaminate, dedicate.*

[265] "As who should say" is equivalent to *as if he were saying,* or *as much as to say.* A frequent usage.—*Cloudy* is *angry, frowning.*—In "turns me his back," *me* is redundant. Often so.—It appears, at the close of scene 4, that Macbeth did not give Macduff a special and direct invitation to the banquet; but his attendance was expected as a matter of course; and his failure to attend made him an object of distrust and suspicion to the tyrant. We are to suppose that Macbeth learned, from the paid spy and informer whom he kept in Macduff's house, that the latter had declared he would not go to the feast. So that the messenger here spoken of was probably not sent to invite Macduff, but to call him to account for his non-attendance, See page 72, notes 253 and 254.

[266] The order is, "our country suffering under a hand accursed."

ACT IV.

SCENE I.

A Cavern. In the middle, a Boiling Caldron.

[*Thunder. Enter the three* WITCHES.]

FIRST WITCH. Thrice the brinded[267] cat hath mew'd.
SECOND WITCH. Thrice; and once[268] the hedge-pig whin'd.
THIRD WITCH. Harpier cries:—'tis time, 'tis time.[269]
FIRST WITCH. Round about the caldron go;
    In the poison'd entrails throw.—
    Toad, that under cold stone,
    Days and nights has thirty-one
    Swelter'd venom sleeping got,
    Boil thou first i' the charmed pot!

[*The* WITCHES *circle the cauldron.*]

ALL. Double, double, toil and trouble;
    Fire, burn; and caldron, bubble.
SECOND WITCH. Fillet of a fenny snake,
    In the caldron boil and bake;
    Eye of newt, and toe of frog,
    Wool of bat, and tongue of dog,
    Adder's fork, and blind-worm's sting,[270]
    Lizard's leg, and howlet's wing,—
    For a charm of powerful trouble,
    Like a hell-broth boil and bubble.
ALL. Double, double, toil and trouble;
    Fire, burn; and caldron, bubble.
THIRD WITCH. Scale of dragon, tooth of wolf,
    Witch's mummy,[271] maw and gulf

---

[267] *Brinded* is but an old form of *brindled*. The colour, as I used to hear it applied to cats and cows, was a dark brown streaked with black.

[268] *Thrice and once* is put for *four*, because, on such occasions, the calling of even numbers was thought unlucky.

[269] Harpy's cry is the signal, showing that it is time to begin their work. *Harpy* is of course a familiar. See page 23, note 2.

[270] *Fork* is put for *forked tongue*. The adder's tongue was thought to have a poisonous sting.—*Blind-worm* is the *slowworm*. Called "eyeless venom'd worm" in *Timon of Athens*, iv. 3.

[271] Probably meaning the mummy of an old Egyptian witch embalmed. Honest mummy was much used as medicine; and a *witch's* of course had evil magic in it. Sir

Of the ravin'd salt-sea shark,[272]
Root of hemlock digg'd i' the dark;[273]
Liver of blaspheming Jew,
Gall of goat, and slips of yew
Sliver'd in the moon's eclipse;[274]
Nose of Turk, and Tartar's lips,
Finger of birth-strangl'd babe
Ditch-deliver'd by a drab,—
Make the gruel thick and slab:
Add thereto a tiger's chaudron,[275]
For the ingredients of our caldron.
ALL. Double, double, toil and trouble;
Fire, burn; and caldron, bubble.
SECOND WITCH. Cool it with a baboon's blood,
Then the charm is firm and good.

[*Enter* HECATE.]

HECATE. O, well done! I commend your pains;
And everyone shall share i' the gains.
And now about the cauldron sing,
Like elves and fairies in a ring,
Enchanting all that you put in.

[*Music and Song, Black spirits, &c.*]

[*Exit* HECATE.]

SECOND WITCH. By the pricking of my thumbs,[276]
Something wicked this way comes:—
Open, locks, whoever knocks!

[*Enter* MACBETH.]

Thomas Browne, in his *Hydriotaphia*, has the following: "The Egyptian mummy, which Cambyses or time hath spared, avarice now consumeth. Mummy is become merchandise, Mizraim cures wounds, and Pharaoh is sold for balsams."

[272] *Ravin* for *ravenous* or *reaming.*—*Maw* is *stomach.*—*Gulf* is *gullet* or *throat*; that which swallows or *gulps down* any thing.

[273] Any poisonous root was thought to become more poisonous if dug on a dark night.

[274] A lunar eclipse was held to be fraught with evil magic of the highest intensity. So in *Paradise Lost*, i. 597: "The Moon in dim eclipse disastrous twilight sheds on half the nations."

[275] *Chaudron* is *entrails.*—*Slab* is *glutinous* or *slabby*; what, in making soft soap, used to be called *ropy.*

[276] I here print just as it is in the original. The song commonly used on the stage is from *The Witch* of Middleton.

MACBETH. How now, you secret, black, and midnight hags!
    What is't you do?
ALL. A deed without a name.
MACBETH. I conjure you, by that which you profess,—
    Howe'er you come to know it,—answer me:
    Though you untie the winds, and let them fight
    Against the churches; though the yesty[277] waves
    Confound and swallow navigation up;
    Though bladed corn be lodged,[278] and trees blown down;
    Though castles topple on their warders' heads;
    Though palaces and pyramids do slope   .
    Their heads to their foundations; though the treasure
    Of nature's germens[279] tumble all together,
    Even till destruction sicken,—answer me
    To what I ask you.
FIRST WITCH. Speak.
SECOND WITCH. Demand.
THIRD WITCH. We'll answer.
FIRST WITCH. Say, if thou'dst rather hear it from our mouths,
    Or from our masters?
MACBETH. Call 'em, let me see 'em.
FIRST WITCH. Pour in sow's blood, that hath eaten
    Her nine farrow;[280] grease that's sweaten
    From the murderer's gibbet throw
    Into the flame.
ALL. Come, high or low;
    Thyself and office deftly[281] show!

[*Thunder. An* APPARITION *of an armed Head rises.*[282]]

MACBETH. Tell me, thou unknown power,—
FIRST WITCH. He knows thy thought:

---

[277] *Yesty* is *foaming, frothy;* like *yeast.*

[278] "*Bladed* corn" is corn *in the blade.—Lodged* is *laid.*

[279] *Germens* are the *seeds,* the springs or principles of *germination,* whether in plants or animals.—"Till destruction sicken" probably means till destruction grows sick of *destroying.*

[280] *Nine farrow* is a *litter of nine pigs. Farrow* is from the Anglo-Saxon *fearh,* which means *give birth to pigs.*

[281] *Deftly* is *adroitly, dexterously.*

[282] The armed head represents symbolically Macbeth's head out off and brought to Malcolm by Macduff. The bloody child is Macduff, untimely ripped from his mother's womb. The child, with a crown on his head and a bough in his hand, is the royal Malcolm, who ordered his soldiers to hew them down a bough, and bear it before them to Dunsinane.—UPTON.

Hear his speech, but say thou nought.[283]
APPARITION. Macbeth! Macbeth! Macbeth! Beware Macduff;
Beware the Thane of Fife.—Dismiss me: enough.[284]

[*Descends.*]

MACBETH. Whate'er thou art, for thy good caution, thanks;
    Thou hast harp'd my fear aright:—but one word more,—
FIRST WITCH. He will not be commanded: here's another,
    More potent than the first.

[*Thunder. An* APPARITION *of a bloody Child rises.*]

APPARITION.—Macbeth! Macbeth! Macbeth!
MACBETH. Had I three ears, I'd hear thee.[285]
APPARITION. Be bloody, bold, and resolute; laugh to scorn
    The power of man, for none of woman born
    Shall harm Macbeth. [*Descends.*]
MACBETH. Then live, Macduff: what need I fear of thee?
    But yet I'll make assurance double sure,
    And take a bond of fate:[286] thou shalt not live;
    That I may tell pale-hearted fear it lies,
    And sleep in spite of thunder.—What is this,

[*Thunder. An* APPARITION *of a Child crowned, with a tree in his*
    hand, rises.]

That rises like the issue of a king,
    And wears upon his baby brow the round
    And top of sovereignty?[287]
ALL. Listen, but speak not to't.
APPARITION. Be lion-mettled, proud; and take no care
    Who chafes, who frets, or where conspirers are:
    Macbeth shall never vanquish'd be, until
    Great Birnam wood to high Dunsínane[288] hill

---

[283] "Silence was necessary during all incantations. So in *The Tempest*: "Be *mute*, or else our spell is marr'd."

[284] Spirits thus evoked were supposed impatient of being questioned.

[285] The meaning probably is, "Had I more ears than I have, I would listen with them all." The stress is on *three*, not on *ears*. So the phrase still in use: "I listened with all the ears I had."

[286] That is, "I will bind fate itself to my cause."

[287] The *round* is that part of a crown which encircles the head: the *top* is the ornament which rises above it, and is symbolical of sovereign power and honour.

[288] The present accent of *Dunsinane* is right. In every other instance the accent is misplaced.

    Shall come against him. [*Descends.*]
MACBETH. That will never be:
    Who can impress the forest;[289] bid the tree
    Unfix his earth-bound root? Sweet bodements, good!
    Rebellion's head, rise never till the wood
    Of Birnam rise, and our high-plac'd Macbeth
    Shall live the lease of nature, pay his breath
    To time and mortal custom.[290] Yet my heart
    Throbs to know one thing: tell me,—if your art
    Can tell so much,—shall Banquo's issue ever
    Reign in this kingdom?
ALL. Seek to know no more.
MACBETH. I will be satisfied: deny me this,
    And an eternal curse fall on you! Let me know:—
    Why sinks that cauldron? and what noise is this? [*Hautboys.*]
FIRST WITCH. Show!
SECOND WITCH. Show!
THIRD WITCH. Show!
ALL. Show his eyes, and grieve his heart;
    Come like shadows, so depart!

    [*Eight* KINGS *appear, and pass over in order, the last with a glass
    in his hand;* BANQUO's *Ghost following.*]

MACBETH. Thou are too like the spirit of Banquo; down!
    Thy crown does sear mine eyeballs:—and thy air,[291]
    Thou other gold-bound brow, is like the first;—
    A third is like the former.—Filthy hags!
    Why do you show me this?—A fourth!—Start, eyes!
    What, will the line stretch out to the crack of doom?
    Another yet!—A seventh!—I'll see no more:—
    And yet the eighth appears, who bears a glass[292]
    Which shows me many more; and some I see

---

[289] "Who can *press* the forest into his service?"

[290] Shall live the full time allotted to man, and then die a natural death.

[291] *Air* for *look* or *appearance*.

[292] The notion of a magic *glass* or charmed mirror, wherein any one might see whatsoever of the distant or the future pertained to himself, seems to have been a part of the old Druidical mythology. There is an allusion to it in *Measure for Measure*, ii. 2: "And, like a prophet, looks in a *glass* that shows what *future evils*," &c. Such was the "brod mirrour of glas" which "the king of Arabic and of Inde" sent to Cambuscan, as related in *The Squieres* Tale of Chaucer. But the most wonderful glass of this kind was that described in *The Faerie Queene*, iii. 2, which

    The great Magitien Merlin had deviz'd
    By his deepe science and hell-dreaded might.

That twofold balls and treble sceptres carry;[293]
Horrible sight!—Now I see 'tis true;
For the blood-bolter'd[294] Banquo smiles upon me,
And points at them for his.—What! is this so?
FIRST WITCH. Ay, sir, all this is so:—but why
Stands Macbeth thus amazedly?—
Come, sisters, cheer we up his sprites,
And show the best of our delights;
I'll charm the air to give a sound,
While you perform your antic round;
That this great king may kindly say,
Our duties did his welcome pay.

[*Music. The* WITCHES *dance, and then vanish.*]

MACBETH. Where are they? Gone?—Let this pernicious hour
Stand aye accursed in the calendar![295]—
Come in, without there!

[*Enter* LENNOX.]

LENNOX. What's your grace's will?
MACBETH. Saw you the weird sisters?
LENNOX. No, my lord.
MACBETH. Came they not by you?
LENNOX. No indeed, my lord.
MACBETH. Infected be the air whereon they ride;
And damn'd all those that trust them!—I did hear
The galloping of horse: who was't came by?
LENNOX. 'Tis two or three, my lord, that bring you word
Macduff is fled to England.
MACBETH. Fled to England!
LENNOX. Ay, my good lord.
MACBETH. [*Aside.*] Time, thou anticipatest[296] my dread exploits:

---

[293] The two balls or globes probably symbolized the two *independent* crowns of England and Scotland; the three sceptres, the kingdoms of England, Scotland, and Ireland. Scott, in *Quentin Durward*, when Charles the Bold has Louis of France in his power, makes Comines say to the King, that "it is his (the Duke's) purpose to close his ducal coronet with an imperial arch, and surmount it with a *globe*, in emblem that his *dominions* are *independent.*"

[294] In Warwickshire, when a horse, sheep, or other animal perspires much, and any of the hair or wool becomes matted into tufts with grime and sweat, he is said to be *boltered*; and whenever the blood issues out and coagulates, forming the locks into hard clotted bunches, the beast is said to be *blood-boltered.*

[295] Alluding to the old custom of marking down *lucky* and *unlucky* days in the almanacs.

The flighty purpose never is o'ertook
Unless the deed go with it: from this moment
The very firstlings of my heart shall be
The firstlings of my hand. And even now,
To crown my thoughts with acts, be it thought and done:
The castle of Macduff I will surprise;
Seize upon Fife; give to the edge o' the sword
His wife, his babes, and all unfortunate souls
That trace him in his line. No boasting like a fool;
This deed I'll do before this purpose cool:
But no more sights!²⁹⁷—Where are these gentlemen?
Come, bring me where they are. [*Exeunt.*]

SCENE II.

Fife. A Room in MACDUFF's *Castle.*

[*Enter* LADY MACDUFF, *her* SON, *and* ROSS.]

LADY MACDUFF. What had he done, to make him fly the land?
ROSS. You must have patience, madam.
LADY MACDUFF. He had none:
His flight was madness: when our actions do not,
Our fears do make²⁹⁸ us traitors.
ROSS. You know not
Whether it was his wisdom or his fear.
LADY MACDUFF. Wisdom! to leave his wife, to leave his babes,
His mansion, and his titles, in a place
From whence himself does fly? He loves us not:
He wants the natural touch:²⁹⁹ for the poor wren,
The most diminutive of birds, will fight,
Her young ones in her nest,³⁰⁰ against the owl.
All is the fear, and nothing is the love;
As little is the wisdom, where the flight
So runs against all reason.
ROSS. My dearest coz,

---

²⁹⁶ The Poet often has *prevent* in the sense of *anticipate*; here he has *anticipate* in the sense of *prevent*.

²⁹⁷ Macbeth does not at all relish the *vision* of Banquo, &c., shown him in the cavern: it vexes and disturbs him greatly. This is evidently what he refers to here.

²⁹⁸ *Make* in the sense of *make out* or *prove*. "When our actions do not convict us of being traitors, our fears do." The Lady is apprehensive that her husband's flight will be construed as proceeding from guilty fear.

²⁹⁹ The sense or sensibility of nature or natural affection. The Poet has "inly *touch* of love" in a like sense.

³⁰⁰ That is, "her young ones *being* in her nest." Ablative absolute.

I pray you, school yourself: but, for your husband,[301]
He is noble, wise, Judicious, and best knows
The fits o' the season.[302] I dare not speak much further:
But cruel are the times, when we are traitors,
And do not know ourselves; when we hold rumour
From what we fear, yet know not what we fear,[303]
But float upon a wild and violent sea
Each way and move. I take my leave of you:
Shall not be long but I'll be here again:
Things at the worst will cease, or else climb upward
To what they were before.[304]—My pretty cousin,
Blessing upon you!

LADY MACDUFF. Father'd he is, and yet he's fatherless.

ROSS. I am so much a fool, should I stay longer,
It would be my disgrace and your discomfort:[305]
I take my leave at once. [*Exit.*]

LADY MACDUFF. Sirrah,[306] your father's dead;
And what will you do now? How will you live?

SON. As birds do, mother.

LADY MACDUFF. What, with worms and flies?

SON. With what I get, I mean; and so do they.

LADY MACDUFF. Poor bird! thou'dst never fear the net nor lime,
The pit-fall nor the gin.[307]

SON. Why should I, mother? Poor birds they are not set for.[308]
My father is not dead, for all your saying.

LADY MACDUFF. Yes, he is dead: how wilt thou do for father?

SON. Nay, how will you do for a husband?

LADY MACDUFF. Why, I can buy me twenty at any market.

SON. Then you'll buy 'em to sell again.

LADY MACDUFF. Thou speak'st with all thy wit; and yet, i' faith,
With wit enough for thee.

SON. Was my father a traitor, mother?

LADY MACDUFF. Ay, that he was.

---

[301] *As to,* or *as regards,* your husband. *For* is often used thus.

[302] The *exigencies* or *dangers* of the time. *Fits* for *turns* or *changes.*

[303] "Fear makes us credit rumour, yet we know not what to fear, because ignorant when we offend." A condition wherein men believe, because they fear, and fear the more, because they cannot foresee the danger.

[304] Meaning, apparently, that, the worse a disease becomes, the sooner there will be either death or recovery. The very excess of an evil often starts a reaction, and thence a return to a better state.

[305] Meaning that he would fall into the *unmanly* act of weeping.

[306] *Sirrah* is here used playfully; perhaps as a note of motherly pride.

[307] *Gin* is *trap* or snare.—*Lime* for *birdlime,* the name of an old device for ensnaring birds.

[308] The bright boy's thought seems to be, that traps are not set for the poor, but for the rich; nor for children, like himself, but for full-grown men.

SON. What is a traitor?

LADY MACDUFF. Why, one that swears and lies.

SON. And be all traitors that do so?

LADY MACDUFF. Everyone that does so is a traitor, and must be hanged.

SON. And must they all be hanged that swear and lie?

LADY MACDUFF. Every one.

SON. Who must hang them?

LADY MACDUFF. Why, the honest men.

SON. Then the liars and swearers are fools: for there are liars and swearers enow to beat the honest men and hang up them.

LADY MACDUFF. Now, God help thee, poor monkey! But how wilt thou do for a father?

SON. If he were dead, you'ld weep for him: if you would not, it were a good sign that I should quickly have a new father.

LADY MACDUFF. Poor prattler, how thou talk'st!

[*Enter a* MESSENGER.[309]]

MESSENGER. Bless you, fair dame! I am not to you known,
　　Though in your state of honour I am perfect.[310]
　　I doubt[311] some danger does approach you nearly:
　　If you will take a homely man's advice,
　　Be not found here; hence, with your little ones.
　　To fright you thus,[312] methinks, I am too savage;
　　To do worse to you were fell cruelty,
　　Which is too nigh your person. Heaven preserve you!
　　I dare abide no longer. [*Exit.*]

LADY MACDUFF. Whither should I fly?
　　I have done no harm. But I remember now
　　I am in this earthly world; where to do harm
　　Is often laudable; to do good sometime
　　Accounted dangerous folly: why then, alas,
　　Do I put up that womanly defence,
　　To say I have done no harm?—What are these faces?

[*Enter* MURDERERS.]

---

[309] This messenger was one of the murderers employed by Macbeth to exterminate Macduff's family; but who, from emotions of remorse and pity, had outstripped his companions, to give timely warning of their approach.—HEATH.

[310] That is, "perfectly acquainted with your honourable rank and character." The Poet has perfect repeatedly so.

[311] Here, as often, *doubt* is used for *fear* or suspect.

[312] "*To fright* you" for *in frightening* you. See page 49, note 142.

FIRST MURDERER. Where is your husband?
LADY MACDUFF. I hope, in no place so unsanctified
  Where such as thou mayst find him.
FIRST MURDERER. He's a traitor.
SON. Thou liest, thou shag-hair'd[313] villain!
FIRST MURDERER. [*Stabbing him.*] What, you egg!
  Young fry of treachery!
SON. He has kill'd me, mother:
  Run away, I pray you![314] [*Dies.*]

    [*Exit* LADY MACDUFF, *crying* Murder! *and pursued by the*
    MURDERERS.]

SCENE III.

England. Before the KING'*s Palace.*

[*Enter* MALCOLM *and* MACDUFF.]

MALCOLM. Let us seek out some desolate shade and there
  Weep our sad bosoms empty.
MACDUFF. Let us rather
  Hold fast the mortal sword, and, like good men,
  Bestride our down-fall'n birthdom.[315] each new morn
  New widows howl; new orphans cry; new sorrows
  Strike heaven on the face, that it resounds
  As if it felt with Scotland, and yell'd out
  Like syllable of dolour.
MALCOLM. What I believe, I'll wail;
  What know, believe; and what I can redress,
  As I shall find the time to friend, I will.
  What you have spoke, it may be so perchance.
  This tyrant, whose sole name blisters our tongues,
  Was once thought honest: you have loved him well;

---

[313] *Shag-hair'd* was a common term of abuse. In Lodge's *Incarnate Devils of this Age*, 1596, we have "*shag-heard* slave."

[314] "This scene," says Coleridge, "dreadful as it is, is still a relief, because a variety, because domestic, and therefore soothing, as associated with the only real pleasures of life. The conversation between Lady Macduff and her child heightens the pathos, and is preparatory for the deep tragedy of their assassination. Shakespeare's fondness for children is everywhere shown: in Prince Arthur in *King John*; in the sweet scene in *The Winter's Tale* between Hermione and her son; nay, even in honest Evans' examination of Mrs. Page's schoolboy."

[315] *Birthdom*, for the place of our birth, our native land. To *bestride* one that was down in battle was a special bravery of friendship.—*Good* here means *brave*. Often so used.

He hath not touch'd you yet. I am young; but something
You may deserve of him through me; and wisdom
To offer up a weak, poor, innocent lamb
To appease an angry god.[316]
MACDUFF. I am not treacherous.
MALCOLM. But Macbeth is.
A good and virtuous nature may recoil
In an imperial charge.[317] But I shall crave your pardon;
That which you are, my thoughts cannot transpose:[318]
Angels are bright still, though the brightest fell:
Though all things foul would wear the brows of grace,
Yet grace must still look so.[319]
MACDUFF. I have lost my hopes.
MALCOLM. Perchance even there where I did find my doubts.[320]
Why in that rawness left you wife and child,
Those precious motives, those strong knots of love,
Without leave-taking? I pray you,
Let not my jealousies be your dishonours,
But mine own safeties: you may be rightly just,
Whatever I shall think.
MACDUFF. Bleed, bleed, poor country!
Great tyranny, lay thou thy basis sure,
For goodness dare not check thee! wear thou thy wrongs,
The title is affeer'd![321]—Fare thee well, lord:
I would not be the villain that thou think'st
For the whole space that's in the tyrant's grasp
And the rich East to boot.
MALCOLM. Be not offended:

---

[316] "You may purchase or secure his favour by sacrificing me to his malice; and to do so would be an act of worldly wisdom on your part, as I have no power to punish you for it."

[317] May recede or fall away from goodness and virtue under the temptation of a man so powerful to resent or to reward.

[318] *Transpose* for *interpret* or *translate*. Not so elsewhere, I think.

[319] That is, though all bad things should counterfeit the looks of goodness, yet goodness must still wear its own looks. *Would* for *should.*

[320] Macduff claims to have fled his home to avoid the tyrant's blow; yet he has left his wife and children in the tyrant's power: this makes the Prince distrust his purpose, and suspect him of being a secret agent of Macbeth. And so, when he says, "I've lost my hopes," the Prince replies, "Perhaps the cause which has destroyed your hopes is the very same that leads me to distrust you; that is, perhaps you have hoped to betray me; which is just what I fear."

[321] Ritson, a lawyer, explains this rightly, no doubt: "To *affeer* is to assess, or reduce to certainty. All amerciaments are, by *Magna Charta*, to be affeered by lawful men, sworn and impartial. This is the ordinary practice of a Court Leet, with which Shakespeare seems to have been intimately acquainted."—In "wear thou thy wrongs," the meaning probably is, wrongs as opposed to *rights*; or, perhaps, place and honours *gained by wrong.*

I speak not as in absolute fear of you.
I think our country sinks beneath the yoke;
It weeps, it bleeds; and each new day a gash
Is added to her wounds. I think, withal,
There would be hands uplifted in my right;
And here, from gracious England,[322] have I offer
Of goodly thousands: but, for all this,
When I shall tread upon the tyrant's head,
Or wear it on my sword, yet my poor country
Shall have more vices than it had before;
More suffer, and more sundry ways than ever,
By him that shall succeed.
MACDUFF. What should he be?
MALCOLM. It is myself I mean: in whom I know
All the particulars of vice so grafted
That, when they shall be open'd, black Macbeth
Will seem as pure as snow; and the poor state
Esteem him as a lamb, being compar'd
With my confineless[323] harms.
MACDUFF. Not in the legions
Of horrid hell can come a devil more damn'd
In evils to top[324] Macbeth.
MALCOLM. I grant him bloody,
Luxurious, avaricious, false, deceitful,
Sudden, malicious, smacking of every sin
That has a name: but there's no bottom, none,
In my voluptuousness: your wives, your daughters,
Your matrons, and your maids, could not fill up
The cistern of my lust; and my desire
All continent[325] impediments would o'erbear,
That did oppose my will: better Macbeth
Than such an one to reign.
MACDUFF. Boundless intemperance
In nature is a tyranny; it hath been
The untimely emptying of the happy throne,
And fall of many kings. But fear not yet
To take upon you what is yours: you may
Convey[326] your pleasures in a spacious plenty,
And yet seem cold, the time you may so hoodwink.

---

[322] Edward the Confessor, who was then King of England.

[323] *Confineless* for *boundless*, or *numberless*. Not so elsewhere.

[324] To *top* is, in old English, to *surpass*.

[325] *Continent* for *restraining* or *holding in*; one of its Latin senses.

[326] To *convey* was sometimes used for to *manage* or *carry through* a thing artfully and secretly.

We have willing dames enough; there cannot be
That vulture in you, to devour so many
As will to greatness dedicate themselves,
Finding it so inclin'd.

MALCOLM. With this there grows,
In my most ill-compos'd affection, such
A stanchless avarice, that, were I king,
I should cut off the nobles for their lands;
Desire his jewels, and this other's house:[327]
And my more-having would be as a sauce
To make me hunger more; that I should forge
Quarrels unjust against the good and loyal,
Destroying them for wealth.

MACDUFF. This avarice
Sticks deeper; grows with more pernicious root
Than summer-seeming lust;[328] and it hath been
The sword of our slain kings:[329] yet do not fear;
Scotland hath foysons to fill up your will,
Of your mere own: all these are portable,
With other graces weigh'd.[330]

MALCOLM. But I have none: the king-becoming graces,
As justice, verity, temperance,[331] stableness,
Bounty, perseverance, mercy, lowliness,
Devotion, patience, courage, fortitude,
I have no relish of them; but abound
In the division[332] of each several crime,
Acting it many ways. Nay, had I power, I should
Pour the sweet milk of concord into hell,
Uproar the universal peace, confound[333]
All unity on earth.

MACDUFF. O Scotland, Scotland!

---

[327] *One man's* jewels and *another man's* house, is the meaning.

[328] Summer-*resembling* lust; the passion that bums awhile like Summer, and like Summer passes away; whereas the other passion, *avarice*, has no such date, but grows stronger and stronger to the end of life. So Donne, in one of his poems, has "a *summer-seeming* Winter's night."

[329] Probably meaning "the sword *that has* slain our kings"; or, perhaps, "the *evil* that has *caused* our kings to be slain with the sword."

[330] *Foison* is an old word for *plenty* or *abundance.—Portable* is *endurable.—Weighed* for *balanced, counterpoised*, or *compensated.—*"Your *mere* own" is *entirely* or *absolutely* your own. *Mere* and *merely* were often used thus.

[331] *Temperance* in its proper Latin sense of *self-restraint*; the opposite of *intemperance* as used a little before.—*Verity* for *veracity.*

[332] *Division* seems to be used here in the sense of *variation*. So it appears to have been sometimes used as a term in music.

[333] A singular use of *uproar*; but probably meaning to *turmoil*, to *fill with tumult* and *uproar.—Confound*, again, for *destroy.*

MALCOLM. If such a one be fit to govern, speak:
I am as I have spoken.
MACDUFF. Fit to govern!
No, not to live!—O nation miserable,
With an untitled tyrant bloody-scepter'd,
When shalt thou see thy wholesome days again,
Since that the truest issue of thy throne
By his own interdiction stands accurs'd
And does blaspheme his breed?—Thy royal father
Was a most sainted king; the queen that bore thee,
Oftener upon her knees than on her feet,
Died every day she lived. Fare-thee-well!
These evils thou repeat'st upon thyself
Have banish'd me from Scotland.—O my breast,
Thy hope ends here!
MALCOLM. Macduff, this noble passion,
Child of integrity, hath from my soul
Wiped the black scruples, reconcil'd my thoughts
To thy good truth and honour. Devilish Macbeth
By many of these trains[334] hath sought to win me
Into his power; and modest wisdom plucks me
From over-credulous haste: but God above
Deal between thee and me! for even now
I put myself to thy direction, and
Unspeak mine own detraction; here abjure
The taints and blames I laid upon myself,
For strangers to my nature. I am yet
Unknown to woman; never was forsworn;
Scarcely have coveted what was mine own;
At no time broke my faith; would not betray
The devil to his fellow;[335] and delight
No less in truth than life: my first false speaking
Was this upon myself. What I am truly,
Is thine and my poor country's to command:
Whither, indeed, before thy here-approach,
Old Siward, with ten thousand warlike men
Already at a point,[336] was setting forth:

---

[334] *Trains* is *arts* or *devices of circumvention. The Edinburgh Review,* October, 1872, shows the word to have been "a technical term both in hawking and hunting: in hawking, for the lure thrown out to reclaim a falcon given to ramble; and in hunting, for the bait trailed along the ground, and left exposed, to tempt the animal from his lair or covert, and bring him fairly within the power of the lurking huntsman."

[335] *Fellow* for *friend* or *companion*; and the sense is, that, if he would not betray the Devil to his friend, much less would he betray him to his enemy. Pretty strong!

[336] *At a point* is *ready, prepared*; or at a stop or period where there is nothing further to be said or done.

Now we'll together; and the chance of goodness
Be like our warranted quarrel![337] Why are you silent?
MACDUFF. Such welcome and unwelcome things at once
'Tis hard to reconcile.

[*Enter a* DOCTOR.]

MALCOLM. Well; more anon.—Comes the king forth, I pray you?
DOCTOR. Ay, sir: there are a crew of wretched souls
That stay his cure: their malady convinces[338]
The great assay of art; but, at his touch,
Such sanctity hath heaven given his hand,
They presently amend.
MALCOLM. I thank you, doctor. [*Exit* DOCTOR.]
MACDUFF. What's the disease he means?
MALCOLM. 'Tis call'd the evil:
A most miraculous work in this good king;
Which often, since my here-remain in England,
I have seen him do. How he solicits heaven,
Himself best knows: but strangely-visited people,
All swoll'n and ulcerous, pitiful to the eye,
The mere[339] despair of surgery, he cures;
Hanging a golden stamp about their necks,
Put on with holy prayers: and 'tis spoken,
To the succeeding royalty he leaves
The healing benediction.[340] With this strange virtue,
He hath a heavenly gift of prophecy;
And sundry blessings hang about his throne,
That speak him full of grace.
MACDUFF. See, who comes here?
MALCOLM. My countryman; but yet I know him not.

[*Enter* ROSS.]

MACDUFF. My ever-gentle cousin, welcome hither.

---

[337] "May the chance for virtue to succeed be as good, as well warranted, as our cause is just." For this use of *quarrel*, see page 24, note 9.

[338] *Convince*, again, in its old sense of *overcome*. See page 43, note 118.

[339] *Mere*, again, for *absolute* or *utter*. See page 88, note 330.

[340] Holinshed has the following respecting Edward the Confessor: "As it has been thought, he was inspired with the gift of prophecy, and also to have the gift of healing infirmities and diseases. He used to help those that were vexed with the disease commonly called the king's evil, and left that virtue as it were a portion of inheritance unto his successors, the kings of this realm." The custom of touching for the king's evil was not wholly laid aside till the days of Queen Anne, who used it on the infant Dr. Johnson.—The *golden stamp* was the coin called *angel*.

MALCOLM. I know him now.[341]—Good God, betimes remove
    The means that makes us strangers!
ROSS. Sir, amen.
MACDUFF. Stands Scotland where it did?
ROSS. Alas, poor country,—
    Almost afraid to know itself! It cannot
    Be call'd our mother, but our grave: where nothing,
    But who knows nothing, is once seen to smile;[342]
    Where sighs, and groans, and shrieks, that rent the air,
    Are made, not mark'd; where violent sorrow seems
    A modern ecstasy:[343] the dead man's knell
    Is there scarce ask'd for who; and good men's lives
    Expire before the flowers in their caps,
    Dying or ere they sicken.
MACDUFF. O, relation
    Too nice,[344] and yet too true!
MALCOLM. What's the newest grief?
ROSS. That of an hour's age doth hiss the speaker;[345]
    Each minute teems a new one.
MACDUFF. How does my wife?
ROSS. Why, well.
MACDUFF. And all my children?
ROSS. Well too.[346]
MACDUFF. The tyrant has not batter'd at their peace?
ROSS. No; they were well at peace when I did leave 'em.
MACDUFF. Be not a niggard of your speech: how goes't?
ROSS. When I came hither to transport the tidings,
    Which I have heavily borne, there ran a rumour
    Of many worthy fellows that were out;[347]
    Which was to my belief witness'd the rather,

---

[341] The Prince at first distrusts Ross, just as he had before distrusted Macduff: but he has given his confidence unreservedly to the latter; and now he has full faith in Ross as soon as he sees how Macduff regards him. The passage is very delightful.—*Means*, next line, is put for *cause*.

[342] Where none but *idiots* and *innocents* are *ever* seen to smile.

[343] *Ecstasy* is any strong *disturbance of mind*. See page 64, note 215.—*Modern* is *common, trite, everyday*; as in the well-known passage, "Full of wise saws and modern instances."

[344] Too *nice*, because too elaborate, or having too much an air of study and art; and so not like the frank utterance of deep feeling.

[345] That which is but an hour old seems out of date, and so *causes* the speaker to be hissed as tedious.

[346] An equivocal phrase, the sense of which is explained in *Antony and Cleopatra*, ii. 5: "We use to say *the dead are well*."

[347] Here *out* has the force of *in arms*, or *in open revolt*.—What follows means that the *rumour* is confirmed by the fact that Macbeth has put his troops in motion.—*For that is because*, or for *the reason* that. Often so.

For that I saw the tyrant's power a-foot:
Now is the time of help; your eye in Scotland
Would create soldiers, make our women fight,
To doff[348] their dire distresses.

MALCOLM. Be't their comfort
We are coming thither: gracious England hath
Lent us good Siward and ten thousand men;
An older and a better soldier none
That Christendom gives out.

ROSS. Would I could answer
This comfort with the like! But I have words
That would be howl'd out in the desert air,
Where hearing should not latch[349] them.

MACDUFF. What concern they?
The general cause? or is it a fee-grief[350]
Due to some single breast?

ROSS. No mind that's honest
But in it shares some woe; though the main part
Pertains to you alone.

MACDUFF. If it be mine,
Keep it not from me, quickly let me have it.

ROSS. Let not your ears despise my tongue for ever,
Which shall possess them with the heaviest sound
That ever yet they heard.

MACDUFF. Humh! I guess at it.

ROSS. Your castle is surpris'd; your wife and babes
Savagely slaughter'd: to relate the manner
Were, on the quarry[351] of these murder'd deer,
To add the death of you.

MALCOLM. Merciful heaven!—
What, man! ne'er pull your hat upon your brows;
Give sorrow words: the grief that does not speak
Whispers the o'er-fraught heart, and bids it break.

MACDUFF. My children too?

ROSS. Wife, children, servants, all
That could be found.

MACDUFF. And I must be from thence!

---

[348] *Doff* is *do off*. So the Poet has *don* for *do on*, and *dup* for *do up*.

[349] Present usage would here transpose *should* and *would*. See page 69, note 237.— *Latch* is an old North-of-England word for *catch*. Our *door-latch* is that which *catches* the door.

[350] A *fee-grief* is a *private* or *individual* grief, as distinguished from one that is public or common.

[351] *Quarry* was a hunter's term for a heap of dead game, and was often applied as here.—In "murder'd *deer*," it may seem that the Poet intended a pun; but probably not; at least I can hardly think he meant the speaker to be conscious of it as such.

My wife kill'd too?

ROSS. I have said.

MALCOLM. Be comforted:

Let's make us medicines of our great revenge,

To cure this deadly grief.

MACDUFF. He has no children.[352]—All my pretty ones?

Did you say all?—O hell-kite!—All?

What, all my pretty chickens and their dam

At one fell swoop[353]?

MALCOLM. Dispute it like a man.

MACDUFF. I shall do so;

But I must also feel it as a man:

I cannot but remember such things were,

That were most precious to me.—Did heaven look on,

And would not take their part? Sinful Macduff,

They were all struck for thee! naught[354] that I am,

Not for their own demerits, but for mine,

Fell slaughter on their souls: heaven rest them now!

MALCOLM. Be this the whetstone of your sword. Let grief

Convert to anger; blunt not the heart, enrage it.

MACDUFF. O, I could play the woman with mine eye,

And braggart with my tongue!—But, gentle heavens,

Cut short all intermission; front to front

Bring thou this fiend of Scotland and myself;

Within my sword's length set him; if he 'scape,

Heaven forgive him too![355]

MALCOLM. This tune goes manly.

Come, go we to the king; our power is ready;

Our lack is nothing but our leave:[356] Macbeth

Is ripe for shaking, and the powers above

---

[352] "He has no children" is most likely said of Malcolm, and with reference to what he has just spoken; though I believe it is commonly taken as referring to Macbeth, and in the idea that, as he has no children, there can be no adequate revenge upon him. But the true meaning, I have no doubt, is, that if Malcolm were a father, he would know that such a grief cannot be healed with the medicine of revenge. Besides, it would seem that Macbeth has children; else why should he strain so hard to have the regal succession "stand in his posterity"? And Lady Macbeth "knows how tender 'tis to love the babe that milks me."

[353] *Swoop* was a term for the descent of a bird of prey upon his quarry.

[354] *Naught* appears to have had the same meaning as *bad*, only stronger. It should not be confounded with *nought*.

[355] The little word *too* is so used here as to intensify, in a very remarkable manner, the sense of what precedes. "Put him once within the reach of my sword, and if I don't kill him, then I am as bad as he, and may God forgive us both!" I cannot point to an instance anywhere of language more intensely charged with meaning.

[356] That is, "nothing remains to be done here but to take our leave of the King." A ceremony of parting.

Put on[357] their instruments. Receive what cheer you may;
The night is long that never finds the day. [*Exeunt.*]

ACT V.

SCENE I.

Dunsinane. A Room in the Castle.

[*Enter a* DOCTOR *of Physic and a* WAITING-GENTLEWOMAN.]

DOCTOR. I have two nights watched with you, but can perceive no truth in your report. When was it she last walked?

GENTLEWOMAN. Since his majesty went into the field,[358] I have seen her rise from her bed, throw her nightgown[359] upon her, unlock her closet, take forth paper, fold it, write upon it, read it, afterwards seal it, and again return to bed; yet all this while in a most fast sleep.

DOCTOR. A great perturbation in nature,—to receive at once the benefit of sleep, and do the effects[360] of watching—In this slumbery agitation, besides her walking and other actual performances, what, at any time, have you heard her say?

GENTLEWOMAN. That, sir, which I will not report after her.

DOCTOR. You may to me; and 'tis most meet you should.

GENTLEWOMAN. Neither to you nor any one; having no witness to confirm my speech. Lo you, here she comes!

[*Enter* LADY MACBETH, *with a taper.*]

This is her very guise; and, upon my life, fast asleep. Observe her; stand close.[361]

DOCTOR. How came she by that light?

GENTLEWOMAN. Why, it stood by her: she has light by her continually; 'tis her command.[362]

---

[357] *Instruments* is here used of *persons.*—*Put on* means *stir up, instigate, urge on.* Often so.

[358] In the preceding scene, Macbeth was said to have his "power a-foot" against "many worthy follows that were out." Probably the coming of the English forces has induced him to withdraw his troops from the field, and put them within the strong fortress of Dunsinane.

[359] That is, *dressing-gown*, not what we call a *night-gown.*

[360] *Effects* here means *acts* or *actions.* Repeatedly so.

[361] Here, again, *close* is *secret, hidden*, or in *concealment.*

[362] Was this to avert the presence of those "sightless substances" once impiously invoked? She seems washing her hands, and "continues in this a quarter of an hour." What a comment on her former boast, "A little water clears us of this deed!"—

DOCTOR. You see, her eyes are open.

GENTLEWOMAN. Ay, but their sense is shut.

DOCTOR. What is it she does now? Look how she rubs her hands.

GENTLEWOMAN. It is an accustomed action with her, to seem thus washing her hands: I have known her continue in this a quarter of an hour.

LADY MACBETH. Yet here's a spot.

DOCTOR. Hark, she speaks: I will set down what comes from her, to satisfy my remembrance the more strongly.

LADY MACBETH. Out, damned spot! out, I say!—One; two; why, then 'tis time to do't.—Hell is murky![363]—Fie, my lord, fie! a soldier, and afeard? What need we fear who knows it, when none can call our power to account?—Yet who would have thought the old man to have had so much blood in him?

DOCTOR. Do you mark that?

LADY MACBETH. The Thane of Fife had a wife; where is she now?—What, will these hands ne'er be clean? No more o' that, my lord, no more o' that: you mar all with this starting.[364]

DOCTOR. Go to, go to; you have known what you should not.

GENTLEWOMAN. She has spoke what she should not, I am sure of that. Heaven knows what she has known.

LADY MACBETH. Here's the smell of the blood still: all the perfumes of Arabia will not sweeten this little hand.[365] Oh, oh, oh!

DOCTOR. What a sigh is there! The heart is sorely charged.

GENTLEWOMAN. I would not have such a heart in my bosom for the dignity of the whole body.

DOCTOR. Well, well, well,—

BUCKNILL.

[363] Some think that Lady Macbeth imagines her husband to utter these words, and repeats them after him with a peculiar intonation as in ridicule or reproach of his fears. And so I suspect it is. But the learned Editors of the "Clarendon Press Series" think otherwise decidedly, and note as follows: "Her recollections of the deed and its motives alternate with recollections of subsequent remorse and dread of future punishment."

[364] She is alluding to the terrors of Macbeth on seeing the Ghost of Banquo in the banquet-scene.

[365] Upon this passage, Verplanck, after remarking how fertile the sense of smell is in the milder and gentler charms of poetry, adds the following: "But the smell has never been successfully used as the means of impressing the imagination with terror, pity, or any of the deeper emotions, except in this dreadful sleep-walking of the guilty Queen, and in one parallel scene of the Greek Drama, as wildly terrible as this. It is that passage of the *Agamemnon* of Æschylus, where the captive prophetess Cassandra, wrapt in visionary inspiration, scents first the smell of blood, and then the vapours of the tomb breathing from the palace of Atrides, as ominous of his approaching murder. These two stand alone in poetry; and Fuseli in his lectures informs us that when, in the kindred art of painting, it has been attempted to produce tragic effect through the medium of ideas drawn from 'this squeamish sense,' even Raphael and Poussin have failed, and excited disgust instead of terror or compassion."

GENTLEWOMAN. Pray God it be, sir.[366]

DOCTOR. This disease is beyond my practice: yet I have known those which have walked in their sleep who have died holily in their beds.

LADY MACBETH. Wash your hands, put on your nightgown; look not so pale:—I tell you yet again, Banquo's buried; he cannot come out on's grave.

DOCTOR. Even so?

LADY MACBETH. To bed, to bed; there's knocking at the gate: come, come, come, come, give me your hand: what's done cannot be undone: to bed, to bed, to bed. [*Exit.*]

DOCTOR. Will she go now to bed?

GENTLEWOMAN. Directly.

DOCTOR. Foul whisperings are abroad: unnatural deeds
Do breed unnatural troubles: infected minds
To their deaf pillows will discharge their secrets.
More needs she the divine than the physician.—
God, God, forgive us all!—Look after her;
Remove from her the means of all annoyance,[367]
And still keep eyes upon her:—so, good-night:
My mind she has mated,[368] and amaz'd my sight:
I think, but dare not speak.

GENTLEWOMAN. Good-night, good doctor. [*Exeunt.*]

---

[366] Does the Gentlewoman misunderstand the Doctor's "Well, well, well," or does she mean this as a further hint how dreadful the thing is? At all events, I have long been wont to pause upon it as one of the Poet's quiet, unobtrusive master-strokes of delineation.

[367] That is, the means of doing violence to herself.

[368] To *mate* or *amate* is to *astonish*, to *strike with dismay*.—It has often struck me as a highly-significant fact, that this scene, which is more intensely tragic than any other in Shakespeare, is all, except the closing speech, written in prose. Why is this? The question is at least not a little curious. The diction is of the very plainest and simplest texture; yet what an impression of sublimity it carries! In fact, I suspect the matter is too sublime, too austerely grand, to admit of any thing so artificial as the measured language of verse, even though the verse were Shakespeare's; and that the Poet, as from an instinct of genius, saw or felt that any attempt to heighten the effect by any such arts or charms of delivery would unbrace and impair it. And I think that the very diction of the closing speech, poetical as it is, must be felt by every competent reader as a letting-down to a lower plane. Is prose, then, after all, a higher form of speech than verse? There are strains in the New Testament which no possible arts of versification could fail to belittle and discrown.

SCENE II.

The Country near Dunsinane.

[*Enter. with drum and colours,* MENTEITH, CAITHNESS,
ANGUS, LENNOX, *and Soldiers.*]

MENTEITH. The English power is near, led on by Malcolm,
His uncle Siward, and the good Macduff.
Revenges burn in them; for their dear causes
Would to the bleeding and the grim alarm
Excite the mortified man.[369]
ANGUS. Near Birnam wood
Shall we well meet them; that way are they coming.
CAITHNESS. Who knows if Donalbain be with his brother?
LENNOX. For certain, sir, he is not: I have a file
Of all the gentry: there is Siward's son
And many unrough[370] youths, that even now
Protest their first of manhood.
MENTEITH. What does the tyrant?
CAITHNESS. Great Dunsinane he strongly fortifies:
Some say he's mad; others, that lesser hate him,
Do call it valiant fury:[371] but, for certain,
He cannot buckle his distemper'd cause
Within the belt of rule.
ANGUS. Now does he feel
His secret murders sticking on his hands;
Now minutely revolts[372] upbraid his faith-breach;
Those he commands move only in command,
Nothing in love: now does he feel his title
Hang loose about him, like a giant's robe
Upon a dwarfish thief.
MENTEITH. Who, then, shall blame
His pester'd senses to recoil and start,[373]
When all that is within him does condemn
Itself for being there?

---

[369] Would rouse and impel even a hermit to the war, to the signal for carnage and horror. By "the *mortified* man" is meant a *religious* man; one who has mortified his passions, is dead to the world.

[370] *Unrough* is *unbearded, smooth-faced.* So in *The Tempest*: "Till newborn chins be *rough* and razorable."

[371] *Fury* in the poetical sense; *inspiration* or *heroic rapture.* So in Hobynoll's lines to Spenser in praise of *The Faerie Queene*: "Some sacred fury hath enrich'd thy brains."

[372] "*Minutely* revolts" are revolts occurring *every minute.*

[373] That is, for *recoiling* and *starting.* See page 84, note 312.

CAITHNESS. Well, march we on,
    To give obedience where 'tis truly ow'd:
    Meet we the medicine of the sickly weal;[374]
    And with him pour we, in our country's purge,
    Each drop of us.
LENNOX. Or so much as it needs,
    To dew the sovereign flower, and drown the weeds.[375]
    Make we our march towards Birnam. [*Exeunt, marching.*]

SCENE III.

Dunsinane. A Room in the Castle.

[*Enter* MACBETH, DOCTOR, *and Attendants.*]

MACBETH. Bring me no more reports; let them fly all:
    Till Birnam wood remove to Dunsinane
    I cannot taint[376] with fear. What's the boy Malcolm?
    Was he not born of woman? The spirits that know
    All mortal consequences have pronounc'd me thus,—
    Fear not, Macbeth; no man that's born of woman
    Shall e'er have power upon thee.—Then fly, false thanes,
    And mingle with the English epicures:[377]
    The mind I sway by, and the heart I bear,
    Shall never sag[378] with doubt nor shake with fear.—

[*Enter a* SERVANT.]

The devil damn thee black, thou cream-fac'd loon! [379]
Where gott'st thou that goose look?
SERVANT. There is ten thousand—
MACBETH. Geese, villain?

---

[374] "The *medicine* of the sickly weal" refers to Malcolm, the lawful Prince. In the olden time, the best remedy for the evils of tyranny, or the greater evils of civil war, was thought to be a king with a clear title.

[375] "Let us shed so much of our blood as may be necessary in order to seat our rightful Prince on the throne, and destroy the usurping tyrant."

[376] To *taint* is to *corrupt*, to *infect*; here used intransitively.

[377] Scotland being a comparatively lean and sterile country, the Scotch might naturally plume themselves on being plain livers and high thinkers, and so speak of the high-feeding English as epicures.

[378] To *sag*, or *swag*, is to hang down by its own weight. "A word," says Mr. Furness, "of every-day use in America among mechanics and engineers." And I can add that I used to hear it often among farmers.

[379] This word, which signifies *a base, abject fellow*, was formerly common in England, but spelt *lown*, and is justly considered by Horne Tooke as the past participle of *to low* or *abase. Lout* has the same origin.

SERVANT. Soldiers, sir.

MACBETH. Go prick thy face and over-red thy fear,
Thou lily-liver'd boy.[380] What soldiers, patch?[381]
Death of thy soul! those linen cheeks of thine
Are counsellors to fear. What soldiers, whey-face?

SERVANT. The English force, so please you.

MACBETH. Take thy face hence. [*Exit Servant.*]
Seyton!—I am sick at heart,
When I behold—Seyton, I say!—This push
Will chair me ever or disseat me now.[382]
I have liv'd long enough: my way of life
Is fall'n into the sere,[383] the yellow leaf;
And that which should accompany old age,
As honour, love, obedience, troops of friends,
I must not look to have; but, in their stead,
Curses, not loud but deep, mouth-honour, breath,
Which the poor heart would fain deny, and dare not.—
Seyton!—

[*Enter* SEYTON.]

SEYTON. What's your gracious pleasure?

MACBETH. What news more?

SEYTON. All is confirm'd, my lord, which was reported.

MACBETH. I'll fight till from my bones my flesh be hack'd.
Give me my armour.

SEYTON. 'Tis not needed yet.

MACBETH. I'll put it on.
Send out more horses, skirr[384] the country round;
Hang those that talk of fear.—Give me mine armour.—
How does your patient, doctor?

DOCTOR. Not so sick, my lord,
As she is troubled with thick-coming fancies,
That keep her from her rest.

---

[380] *Lily-liver'd, white-liver'd, milk-liver'd*, were all strong words for *cowardly*.

[381] *Patch* was often used as a term of contempt. The use probably grew from the motley or *patch-work* dress worn by professional Fools.

[382] "Will *seat* me firmly on the throne, or else will *unseat* me utterly." If he whip the present enemy, his tenure of the crown will be confirmed; if he fail now, there will be no more hope for him.

[383] *Sere* is *dry, withered*. Often so used.—"Way of life" is merely an enlarged expression for *life*. Macbeth's complaint is, that he is now growing old, and that he cannot expect to have the natural comforts of old age.

[384] *Skirr* is an old word for *scour*, and has the sense of *moving swiftly*. So in *King Henry V.*, iv. 7: "And make them *skirr* away, as swift as stones enforced from the old Assyrian slings."

MACBETH. Cure her of that:
    Canst thou not minister to a mind diseas'd;
    Pluck from the memory a rooted sorrow;
    Raze out the written troubles of the brain;
    And with some sweet oblivious antidote
    Cleanse the stuff'd bosom of that perilous stuff
    Which weighs upon the heart?
DOCTOR. Therein the patient
    Must minister to himself.
MACBETH. Throw physic to the dogs,—I'll none of it.—
    Come, put mine armour on; give me my staff.[385]—
    Seyton, send out.—Doctor, the Thanes fly from me.—
    Come, sir, despatch.—If thou couldst, doctor, cast
    The water of my land,[386] find her disease,
    And purge it to a sound and pristine health,
    I would applaud thee to the very echo,
    That should applaud again.—Pull't off, I say.[387]—
    What rhubarb, senna, or what purgative drug,
    Would scour these English hence? Hear'st thou of them?
DOCTOR. Ay, my good lord; your royal preparation
    Makes us hear something.
MACBETH. Bring it[388] after me.—
    I will not be afraid of death and bane,
    Till Birnam forest come to Dunsinane.

[*Exeunt all except* DOCTOR.]

DOCTOR. Were I from Dunsinane away and clear,
    Profit again should hardly draw me here. [*Exit.*]

---

[385] *Staff* probably means his symbol of military command; general's *baton*. Or it may mean a fighting-tool; his *lance*.

[386] Probably alluding to the old custom of medical diagnosis by inspecting or *casting* the patient's water. So that the language is equivalent to "*diagnosticate* all the people of Scotland."

[387] Spoken to the armourer, who has got a piece of the armour on wrong.

[388] Referring to the piece which he has just ordered the armourer to pull off.

SCENE IV.

Country near Dunsinane: a Wood in view.

[*Enter, with drum and colours*, MALCOLM, *old* SIWARD
and his SON, MACDUFF, MENTEITH, CAITHNESS,
ANGUS, LENNOX, ROSS, *and Soldiers, marching.*]

MALCOLM. Cousins, I hope the days are near at hand
    That chambers will be safe.[389]
MENTEITH. We doubt it nothing.
SIWARD. What wood is this before us?
MENTEITH. The wood of Birnam.
MALCOLM. Let every soldier hew him down a bough,
    And bear't before him; thereby shall we shadow
    The numbers of our host, and make discovery
    Err in report of us.
SOLDIERS. It shall be done.
SIWARD. We learn no other but the confident tyrant
    Keeps still in Dunsinane, and will endure
    Our setting down before't.
MALCOLM. 'Tis his main hope:
    For where there is advantage to be given,
    Both more and less[390] have given him the revolt;
    And none serve with him but constrained things,
    Whose hearts are absent too.
MACDUFF. Let our just censures
    Attend the true event,[391] and put we on
    Industrious soldiership.
SIWARD. The time approaches,
    That will with due decision make us know
    What we shall say we have, and what we owe.[392]
    Thoughts speculative their unsure hopes relate;
    But certain issue strokes must arbitrate:[393]

---

[389] Referring, probably, to the spies and informers whom Macbeth keeps in the noblemen's houses, prowling about their private chambers, and listening at their key-holes. See page 72, note 254.

[390] *More and less* is the old phrase for *great and small*, or *high and low.*

[391] Another proleptical form of speech; the meaning being, "Let our judgments wait for the actual result, the issue of the contest, *in order that they may be* just." See page 70, note 240.

[392] Evidently meaning, "When we have a king that will rule by law we shall know both our rights and our duties." I make this note simply because some have vented an unworthy sneer, not indeed at the Poet, but at the brave old warrior for speaking thus.

[393] Referring, apparently, to Malcolm's last speech, which proceeds somewhat upon

Towards which advance the war. [*Exeunt, marching.*]

SCENE V.

Dunsinane. Within the castle.

[*Enter with drum and colours,* MACBETH, SEYTON, *and Soldiers.*]

MACBETH. Hang out our banners on the outward walls;
    The cry is still, *They come.* our castle's strength
    Will laugh a siege to scorn: here let them lie
    Till famine and the ague eat them up:
    Were they not forced[394] with those that should be ours,
    We might have met them dareful, beard to beard,
    And beat them backward home.—[*A cry of women within.*]
        What is that noise?
SEYTON. It is the cry of women, my good lord. [*Exit.*]
MACBETH. I have almost forgot the taste of fears:
    The time has been, my senses would have cool'd
    To hear a night-shriek; and my fell[395] of hair
    Would at a dismal treatise[396] rouse and stir
    As life were in't: I have supp'd full with horrors;
    Direness, familiar to my slaught'rous thoughts,
    Cannot once start me.

    [*Re-enter* SEYTON.]

    Wherefore was that cry?
SEYTON. The queen, my lord, is dead.
MACBETH. She should have died hereafter;
    There would have been a time for such a word.[397]

---

conjecture and seeming likelihood. The old war-horse means, "There's no use in talking about it, and eating the air of expectation; nothing but plain old-fashioned fighting will decide the matter."

[394] *Forced* is *strengthened, reinforced.* A frequent usage.

[395] *Fell* is *hairy scalp,* or any skin covered with hair or wool.—*To hear* is still another gerundial infinitive; *at hearing.*

[396] *Dismal treatise* probably means a tale of cruelty, or of suffering.

[397] Another instance of the indiscriminate use of *should* and *would*; and the meaning is, "If she had not died now, she *would* have died hereafter; the time would have come when such a word must be spoken." The explanation of the whole passage comes to me well worded from Mr. Joseph Crosby; though the substance of it was put forth many years ago by the Rev. Mr. Arrowsmith: "'I used to be frightened out of my senses at almost any thing: now nothing—not even the most terrible calamities—can make any impression upon me. What *must* be, I know *will* be.' 'The Queen, my lord, is dead.' 'Well, be it so: had she not died *now*, she would have had to die some time. So creeps along every thing in the world, with petty pace from day to day: every to-morrow has its

To-morrow, and to-morrow, and to-morrow,
Creeps in this petty pace from day to day,
To the last syllable of recorded time;[398]
And all our yesterdays have lighted fools
The way to dusty death. Out, out, brief candle!
Life's but a walking shadow; a poor player,
That struts and frets his hour upon the stage,
And then is heard no more: it is a tale
Told by an idiot, full of sound and fury,
Signifying nothing.[399]—

[*Enter a* MESSENGER.]

Thou comest to use thy tongue; thy story quickly.
MESSENGER. Gracious my lord,
I should report that which I say I saw,
But know not how to do it.
MACBETH. Well, say, sir.
MESSENGER. As I did stand my watch upon the hill,
I look'd toward Birnam, and anon, methought,
The wood began to move.
MACBETH. Liar, and slave!
MESSENGER. Let me endure your wrath, if't be not so.
Within this three mile may you see it coming;
I say, a moving grove.
MACBETH. If thou speak'st false,
Upon the next tree shalt thou hang alive,
Till famine cling[400] thee: if thy speech be sooth,
I care not if thou dost for me as much.—
I pall[401] in resolution; and begin
To doubt the equivocation of the fiend
That lies like truth. *Fear not, till Birnam wood*
Do come to Dunsinane; and now a wood
Comes toward Dunsinane.—Arm, arm, and out!—

---

yesterday, and every yesterday its to-morrow; and thus men go on from yesterdays to to-morrows, like automatic fools, until they drop into the dusty grave.'"

[398] "The last syllable of *recorded* time" means simply the last syllable of the record of time. Such proleptical forms of speech are uncommonly frequent in this play.

[399] Alas for Macbeth! Now all is inward with him; he has no more prudential prospective reasonings. His wife, the only being who could have had any seat in his affections, dies: he puts on despondency, the final heart-armour of the wretched, and would fain think every thing shadowy and unsubstantial; as indeed all things are to those who cannot regard them as symbols of goodness.—COLERIDGE.

[400] To *cling*, in the northern counties, signifies to *shrivel, wither*, or *dry up. Clung-wood* is wood of which the sap is entirely dried or spent.

[401] To *pall* is to *droop*, to *fall away*, to *languish*, to *grow faint.*

If this which he avouches does appear,
There is nor flying hence nor tarrying here.
I 'gin to be a-weary of the sun,
And wish the estate o' the world were now undone.—
Ring the alarum bell!—Blow, wind! come, wrack!
At least we'll die with harness[402] on our back. [*Exeunt.*]

SCENE VI.

The Same. A Plain before the Castle.

[*Enter, with drum and colours,* MALCOLM, *old* SIWARD,
MACDUFF, *&c., and their Army, with boughs.*]

MALCOLM. Now near enough; your leafy screens throw down,
And show like those you are.—You, worthy uncle,
Shall with my cousin, your right-noble son,
Lead our first battle:[403] worthy Macduff and we
Shall take upon's what else remains to do,
According to our order.
SIWARD. Fare you well.—
Do we but find the tyrant's power to-night,
Let us be beaten, if we cannot fight.
MACDUFF. Make all our trumpets speak; give them all breath,
Those clamorous harbingers of blood and death. [*Exeunt.*]

SCENE VII.

The Same. Another part of the Plain.

[*Alarums. Enter* MACBETH.]

MACBETH. They have tied me to a stake; I cannot fly,
But, bear-like I must fight the course.[404] What's he
That was not born of woman? Such a one
Am I to fear, or none.

[*Enter young* SIWARD.]

YOUNG SIWARD. What is thy name?

---

[402] *Harness* for *armour*. Repeatedly so.
[403] *Battle* was often put for *army* in *battle-array*: here it is put, apparently, for a *part* of such an army; the *van*.
[404] This was a phrase of bear-baiting, where the bear was tied to a stake, and then the dogs set upon him: the poor bear could not run, and so had no way but to fight it out.

MACBETH. Thou'lt be afraid to hear it.
YOUNG SIWARD. No; though thou call'st thyself a hotter name
    Than any is in hell.
MACBETH. My name's Macbeth.
YOUNG SIWARD. The devil himself could not pronounce a title
    More hateful to mine ear.
MACBETH. No, nor more fearful.
YOUNG SIWARD. Thou liest, abhorred tyrant; with my sword
    I'll prove the lie thou speak'st.

    [*They fight, and young* SIWARD *is slain.*]

MACBETH. Thou wast born of woman.—
    But swords I smile at, weapons laugh to scorn,
    Brandish'd by man that's of a woman born. [*Exit.*]

    [*Alarums. Enter* MACDUFF.]

MACDUFF. That way the noise is.—Tyrant, show thy face!
    If thou be'st slain and with no stroke of mine,
    My wife and children's ghosts will haunt me still.
    I cannot strike at wretched kerns, whose arms
    Are hired to bear their staves; either thou, Macbeth,
    Or else my sword, with an unbatter'd edge,
    I sheathe again undeeded. There thou shouldst be;
    By this great clatter, one of greatest note
    Seems bruited.[405] Let me find him, fortune!
    And more I beg not. [*Exit. Alarums.*]

    [*Enter* MALCOLM *and old* SIWARD.]

SIWARD. This way, my lord;—the castle's gently render'd:
    The tyrant's people on both sides do fight;
    The noble thanes do bravely in the war;
    The day almost itself professes yours,
    And little is to do.
MALCOLM. We have met with foes
    That strike beside us.[406]
SIWARD. Enter, sir, the castle. [*Exeunt. Alarums.*]

---

[405] *Bruited* is *reported, noised* abroad.—Of course, wherever Macbeth goes, he has a strong escort attending him; and the clattering of so many feet and swords would indicate his approach.

[406] "Foes who take pains not to hit us; who are only shamming fight against us, while their hearts are on our side."

SCENE VIII.

The Same. Another part of the field.

[*Enter* MACBETH.]

MACBETH. Why should I play the Roman fool, and die
    On mine own sword?[407] whiles I see lives, the gashes
    Do better upon them.[408]

[*Enter* MACDUFF.]

MACDUFF. Turn, hell-hound, turn!
MACBETH. Of all men else I have avoided thee:
    But get thee back; my soul is too much charg'd
    With blood of thine already.
MACDUFF. I have no words,—
    My voice is in my sword: thou bloodier villain
    Than terms can give thee out! [*They fight.*]
MACBETH. Thou losest labour:
    As easy mayst thou the intrenchant[409] air
    With thy keen sword impress, as make me bleed:
    Let fall thy blade on vulnerable crests;
    I bear a charmed life,[410] which must not yield
    To one of woman born.
MACDUFF. Despair thy charm;
    And let the angel whom thou still hast serv'd
    Tell thee, Macduff was from his mother's womb
    Untimely ripp'd.
MACBETH. Accursed be that tongue that tells me so,
    For it hath cow'd my better part of man!
    And be these juggling fiends no more believ'd,
    That palter[411] with us in a double sense;
    That keep the word of promise to our ear,
    And break it to our hope!—I'll not fight with thee.
MACDUFF. Then yield thee, coward,

---

[407] Probably alluding either to the suicide of Cato at Utica or that of Brutus at Philippi; perhaps to both.

[408] "While I see *living foes*, it is better to kill them than myself."

[409] To *trench* is to *cut*, to *wound*, so that *intrenchant* is *invulnerable*; literally, *uncuttable*.

[410] "A *charmed* life" is a life secured against human assault by "the might of magic spells."

[411] To *palter* is to *shuffle* or *equivocate*, to *haggle* or *dodge*. Often so.

And live to be the show and gaze o' the time:
We'll have thee, as our rarer monsters are,
Painted upon a pole, and underwrit,
Here may you see the tyrant.[412]

MACBETH. I will not yield,
To kiss the ground before young Malcolm's feet,
And to be baited[413] with the rabble's curse.
Though Birnam wood be come to Dunsinane,
And thou oppos'd, being of no woman born,
Yet I will try the last. Before my body
I throw my warlike shield: lay on, Macduff;
And damn'd be him that first cries, *Hold, enough!*[414]

[*Exeunt fighting.*]

[*Retreat. Flourish. Enter, with drum and colours,* MALCOLM, *old*
SIWARD, ROSS, LENNOX, ANGUS, CAITHNESS,
MENTEITH, *and Soldiers.*]

MALCOLM. I would the friends we miss were safe arriv'd.
SIWARD. Some must go off:[415] and yet, by these I see,
So great a day as this is cheaply bought.
MALCOLM. Macduff is missing, and your noble son.
ROSS. Your son, my lord, has paid a soldier's debt:
He only liv'd but till he was a man;
The which no sooner had his prowess confirm'd
In the unshrinking station where he fought,[416]
But like a man he died.
SIWARD. Then he is dead?
FLEANCE. Ay, and brought off the field: your cause of sorrow
Must not be measur'd by his worth, for then
It hath no end.
SIWARD. Had he his hurts before?
ROSS. Ay, on the front.

---

[412] Alluding to the Barnum practice of the time; which was, to get some strange animal for a show, and then hang out an exaggerated painting of the beast to attract customers.

[413] *Baited* is *barked* at or *worried*, as dogs worried a chained bear.

[414] To cry *hold!* when persons were fighting, was an authoritative way of separating them, according to the old military laws. This is shown by a passage in Bellay's *Instructions for the Wars*, declaring it to be a capital offence, "Whosoever shall strike stroke at his adversary, either in the heat or otherwise, if a third do cry *hold*, to the intent to part them." This illustrates the passage in i. 5, of this play: "Nor Heaven peep through the blanket of the dark *to cry Hold! hold!*"

[415] The meaning is, that in such a contest some must *be killed* of course.

[416] That is, the *place* where he fought *without shrinking.*

SIWARD. Why then, God's soldier be he!
 Had I as many sons as I have hairs,
 I would not wish them to a fairer death:
 And, so his knell is knoll'd.
MALCOLM. He's worth more sorrow,
 And that I'll spend for him.
SIWARD. He's worth no more:
 They say he parted well, and paid his score:[417]
 And so, God be with him!—Here comes newer comfort.

  [*Re-enter* MACDUFF, *with* MACBETH's *head.*]

MACDUFF. Hail, king, for so thou art: behold, where stands
 The usurper's cursed head: the time is free:
 I see thee compass'd with thy kingdom's pearl,[418]
 That speak my salutation in their minds;
 Whose voices I desire aloud with mine,—
 Hail, King of Scotland!
ALL. Hail, King of Scotland! [*Flourish.*]
MALCOLM. We shall not spend a large expense of time
 Before we reckon with your several loves,
 And make us even with you. My thanes and kinsmen,
 Henceforth be earls, the first that ever Scotland
 In such an honour named.[419] What's more to do,
 Which would be planted newly with the time,—
 As calling home our exil'd friends abroad,[420]
 That fled the snares of watchful tyranny;
 Producing forth the cruel ministers
 Of this dead butcher, and his fiend-like queen,—

---

 [417] To *part* and to *depart* were used indiscriminately. The allusion is to a traveller taking leave of an inn.—*Score* is *account* or *bill*. Tavern accounts were commonly kept either by marking down the items with chalk on a board, or by notches cut, *scored*, in a stick.—This little episode of old Siward and his son is taken from Holinshed: "It is recorded also, that in the foresaid battell, in which earle Siward vanquished the Scots, one of Siwards sonnes chanced to be slaine, whereof although the father had good cause to be sorrowfull, yet when he heard that he died of a wound which he had receiued in fighting stoutlie in the forepart of his bodie, and that with his face towards the enemie, he greatlie rejoised thereat, to heare that he died so manfullie."

 [418] *Pearl* is here a collective noun, and equivalent to *jewels*. The metaphor is of a string of pearls encircling the neck, or the head, of royalty. Just the right thing to be said of the brave men who have vindicated Malcolm's title, and rid their country of the butchering tyrant. Milton has a like use of pearl: "But this is got by casting pearl to hogs."

 [419] Malcolm, immediately after his coronation, called a parliament at Forfair; in the which he rewarded them with lands and livings that had assisted him against Macbeth. Manie of them that were before *thanes* were at this time made *earles*; as Fife, Menteith, Atholl, Levenox, Murrey, Caithness, Rosse, and Angus.—HOLINSHED.

 [420] "Friends exiled abroad" is the natural order of the words.

Who, as 'tis thought, by self and violent hands
Took off her life;—this, and what needful else
That calls upon us, by the grace of Grace,
We will perform in measure, time, and place:
So, thanks to all at once, and to each one,
Whom we invite to see us crown'd at Scone. [*Flourish. Exeunt.*]

THE END

Made in the USA
San Bernardino, CA
24 July 2020